COUNTRY DECORATING through the seasons

Over 130 step-by-step projects and inspirational ideas

Deborah Schneebeli-Morrell and Gloria Nicol

Checkmark Books™
An imprint of Facts On File, Inc.

Country Decorating through the Seasons

Copyright © Collins & Brown Limited 1999
Text copyright © Collins & Brown Limited 1999
Photographs copyright © Collins & Brown Limited 1999

First published in Great Britain in 1999
by Collins & Brown Limited
London House
Great Eastern Wharf
Parkgate Road
London SW11 4NQ

Facts On File, Inc.
11 Penn Plaza
New York NY 10001

ISBN 0-8160-4015-X (HC)
ISBN 0-8160-4050-8 (PB)

Facts On File books are available at special discounts when purchased in
bulk quantities for businesses, associations, institutions or sales promotions.
Please call our Special Sales Department in New York at (212) 967-8800 or
(800) 322-8755.

You can find Facts On File on the World Wide Web at http://www.factsonfile.com

Editor: Gillian Haslam
Designer: Roger Daniels
Photographer: Gloria Nicol
Stylists: Deborah Schneebeli-Morrell and Gloria Nicol

Reproduction by Grafiscan SRL, Italy
Printed and bound in China

10 9 8 7 6 5 4 3 2 1

Authors' Acknowledgments
The authors would like to thank kind friends who lent their homes and
gardens as locations for this book: Jill Patchett and Alan Du Monceau in
Gloucestershire, Mary MacCarthy in Norfolk and Julie Hailey in London.
Very special thanks are due to Emma Hardy for her hard work and creative
support with some of the projects and to Jim Nicol who provided us with
delicious and sustaining cakes. A very special thank you to our long-
suffering editor Gillian Haslam, who skillfully and diplomatically kept us
going and supported us throughout this long project. Lastly, a big thank
you to Cindy Richards, editorial director at Collins & Brown, who chose
us as a team to produce this book.

*For my friends
Jill Patchett and Alan Du Monceau*

Deborah Schneebeli-Morrell

*"Take the thing that lies nearest,
shape from that your work of art"
For Gabrielle Ryves*

Gloria Nicol

CONTENTS

INTRODUCTION 6

INTRODUCTION

As time rushes by in a busy world, it is all too easy to miss the individual atmosphere of each season that can so enrich our lives. It is only when we pay particular attention to the quality of each season that we are enabled to live in the present. We really have to savor each moment to avoid the feeling of life running away with us, and we can do this by exploiting the natural world. Appreciating the passing of the seasons is one of the most rewarding human experiences, and our rich heritage of music, art and poetry is a testament to that. Much of our appreciation of the living world, of flowers, landscapes and trees, is directly related to having read a poem or seen a painting through the eyes of an artist. It has a way of drawing our attention to the detail in nature, and consequently to the individual quality of each season.

Early spring brings the excitement of seeing the first crocus push its timid head through the thawing snow. Innocent primroses and shy violets miraculously appear, and long dormant buds swell and burst into new life. Although the air can still be crisp and cool, the days are gradually lengthening, and the new light has a brightness in contrast to the sometimes gray days of winter. It is the first opportunity for children to rush outside and expend some of their pent-up energy and with Easter approaching, eggs can be decorated and little nests containing the enticing chocolate variety can be hidden around the garden for the Easter egg hunt. As warm days become more common, it is fun to arrange a children's tea party under the blossom-laden boughs of an apple tree. This is the time for planning the year ahead, for planting and sowing seed. Full of optimism, the energy of the season is reflected in our human activity.

LEFT: *Tight clusters of sweetly scented springtime grape hyacinths look best arranged in a generous bunch in a pretty fluted tin.*

RIGHT: *The elder tree provides us with fragrant blossoms from early summer onward. This is used to make unusual yet delicious fritters, as well as a refreshing cordial.*

LEFT: *Autumn is the time for preserving and bottling the fruits and produce of the garden.*

RIGHT: *When Christmas is finally upon us, the whole family can enjoy the age-old tradition of decorating the Christmas tree.*

where meals can be taken well into the dusk of evening, giving us an opportunity to create pretty lanterns and lights to extend the party into the night when the most fragrant plants give out their scent for pollination. Thoughts turn to seaside holidays, a whole world in itself, creating an atmosphere of gentle nostalgia as childhood scenes are remembered.

As the days gradually shorten, the summer plants are past their best and the temperature dips, encouraging leaves to take on the fiery hues of autumn, from amber, russet and ocher to an inky purple. Our first taste of the autumn harvest often comes after the first gusts of wind blow the ripening apples to the ground. As autumn gives up its fruit, this is the traditional time for gathering in the harvest, for making preserves and bottling fruit to tide us through the months ahead. While tidying the garden we gather seeds and start to plan for the year to come. Pumpkins and squash are picked before the frosts arrive and are carved into spooky lanterns for Halloween. Vermilion rosehips, sloes, trailing bryony, wild clematis and the last of the

As spring gently breaks into summer, at first tentatively and later with an explosion of growth, color and scent, we feel the need to take a break from the normal pace of life. Work in the garden becomes a welcome relaxation and a time when we invent new planting schemes for the garden or the window box. The long, drawn out days encourage outdoor living, with the house extending into the garden and the garden offering up its many gifts to the house in the form of beautiful flowers and abundant vegetables and soft fruit. A table can be set permanently outside

blackberries mark the last flush of abundance before winter sets in.

The chill in the air when winter arrives makes us shudder; we draw inside and wonder how we will survive the long cold season. The fields are fallow and the leafless trees are silhouetted against a harsh sky. The weather deepens, snow falls on the barren landscape, welcoming log fires are lit to keep us warm and we raise our spirits by entertaining friends and family. At last we have the joyful festivity of Christmas to look forward to. We can be at our most creative now, cooking and baking, making sweets and wrapping presents for the inevitable parties, decorating the home and, best of all, bringing in the Christmas tree with its foresty fragrance to make a focal point in the center of the home. Take a little extra time to add to a treasured collection of handed-down tree ornaments. The house radiates warmth and pleasure, it glitters and glows. The new year fast approaches and we welcome its promise with a host of new resolutions. The cycle starts all over again and we know that this year will be better than the last.

SPRING

Spring Flowers

AT LAST THE LONG WINTER IS OVER, the garden is full of promise and once again it is possible to pick armfuls of scented blossom for the home. Drifts of golden daffodils give way to stately tulips, which, in turn, give up their blowsy heads to the swaying blossom of the lilac trees. A traditional country favorite with an intoxicating scent, lilac lasts well when cut.

Blossoms and Bulbs

ABOVE: *Giant hyacinths are generous with their fragrance. Almost too formal to be grown in a flowerbed, they look their best in plain containers, such as these galvanized metal pots in a fluted shape.*

ABOVE: *The primrose is one of the earliest heralds of spring when its yellow delicate flowers appear. They are perfect for the garden as they can tolerate most conditions and spread rapidly. Plant a few clumps in baskets and bring them inside; they will happily return to the garden when their flowering period is over.*

LEFT: *Lacy cow parsley is one of the prettiest meadow flowers and can be grown in the garden as a cultivated flower. The flowers drop quickly, but don't let that deter you.*

RIGHT: *This posy of bluebells, campion, forget-me-nots and sweet rocket needs no fancy vase — just tie with a simple length of colored ribbon.*

BELOW: *Apple blossom looks delightful tumbling over the rim of a wicker basket. To keep the flowers fresh, line the base of the basket with plastic and pack in blocks of florists' foam soaked in water. This also makes it easier to arrange the flowers, as stems can be pushed into the foam. Keep the foam moist, and the blossom will last a long time.*

ABOVE: *These tightly packed bunches of grape hyacinths are displayed in a row of tiny fluted tin molds, the color of which subtly complements the beautiful range of blue shades in the flower heads.*

RIGHT: *Pick branches of chestnut or cherry just as their buds are beginning to swell. Bring them inside to the warmth of the house and they will burst into blossom, giving a special preview of spring.*

SPRING WREATH

A WREATH DECKED with the produce of the season captures the spirit of springtime and provides a welcoming flourish when used to decorate your front door. The base is covered with green carpet moss to provide a lush velvet surface to decorate. Speckled quails' eggs and raffia-tied bundles of pussy willow continue the nature trail theme, with small bunches of primroses adding a splash of color. Display the wreath in a cool place and spray it regularly with water to help it to stay fresh. If using freshly cut flowers, push the stem ends into the damp moss.

1 Soak the sphagnum moss in a bucket of water, then squeeze out any excess water. Bind handfuls of the damp moss to the wreath frame with garden twine.

2 Cover the sphagnum moss ring with clumps of carpet moss, butting the pieces together and fixing them in place with pins made from short lengths of florist wire bent into U shapes.

4 Tie the pussy willow into small bundles with several strands of raffia. Attach a florist wire to the back of each bundle, leaving a long end. Arrange the bundles around the wreath, pushing the wires through to the back and securing as before.

3 Glue florist wires to the blown quails' eggs using a glue gun. Arrange the eggs in groups around the wreath base and push the wires through to the back, winding them around the wreath frame to secure. Trim the wire ends.

5 Make small bunches of primroses and incorporate a leaf or two into each one. Wrap a length of wire around each one and arrange them among the eggs and twigs, pushing the wires through to the back and securing. Attach a wire hanging loop to the back of the wreath.

PRIMROSE WRAPPING PAPER

POTATO PRINTING is a favorite, uncomplicated technique familiar to most people from their first days at school. An infinitely adaptable craft that has many applications, this type of printing can be done on wood, metal, paper and fabric. It is one of the simplest ways of making a repetitive pattern and can be used on a small or large scale. Here the primrose, that welcome spring flower, has been used as the motif and the combination of this image and the natural plant paper makes an ideal book jacket for a garden notebook.

To cover a book, lay the open book on the printed paper. Cut the paper to fit, leaving a 2 in (5 cm) margin all around. Bend this margin around the book covers and stick neatly in position using double-sided tape to hold it firmly in place. A smaller margin needs to be cut at the spine so it can be tucked in and stuck in place.

YOU WILL NEED

Templates (see page 184)

Scissors

Two potatoes, one round and one long

Kitchen knife

Selection of natural-fiber papers (large enough to wrap around a notebook of your choice)

Water-soluble crayon

Two paint brushes

Yellow and green acrylic paints

Mixing palette or old plate

1 Draw a simple flower and leaf template onto cardboard and cut out. Cut the potatoes carefully in half with one clean cut each. Place the template onto the moist cut surface and draw around it with water-soluble crayon.

2 Remove the templates and cut down neatly around the leaf and flower shapes, making short, vertical cuts with the knife. Cut away the surplus by slicing into the potato from the side, meeting the downward cut. Make the veins in the leaf by making tight V-shaped cuts. It is important to cut away the design neatly to create an even design.

3 Mix the paint with water to make a creamy consistency and apply evenly to the potato with the brush. Only apply paint to the leaf design at this stage.

4 Turn the potato over and press it firmly and evenly down onto the sheet of plant paper. This has been placed on a sheet of scrap paper to protect the work surface. Starting from the top of the long side of the sheet approximately 4¾ in (12 cm) in from the edge, print your design in leaf pairs.

5 Print more strips of leaves across the paper, remembering to leave enough space between each strip to print the flower shape. Apply watered down yellow paint to the flower shape and print a line of six flowers between each row of leaves. Allow the paper to dry.

Breakfast in Bed

ONE OF LIFE'S GREAT PLEASURES is to receive breakfast in bed. In a hectic world this is a rare treat, but on a weekend spring morning, when the air is still cool outside and the changing quality of light heralds the fast-approaching summer, staying in a bed a little longer, perhaps with freshly made coffee and a light breakfast, along with the morning papers, is wise and can set you in a pleasant, relaxed mood for the whole day. Somehow even more pleasure is derived from being the one to treat a special houseguest by delivering breakfast in bed on a pretty, high-sided tray.

PAPER CUTOUT TRAY

THIS STRIKING TRAY, perfect for a leisurely breakfast in bed, is decorated with a design inspired by traditional Polish papercutting. This rewarding country craft employs the use of folded and cut paper, resulting in a satisfyingly symmetrical design. The simple stylized imagery usually relates to subjects and events in everyday rural life and therefore often has a symbolic quality. The tree of life, as used on the tray shown in this project, is a favorite theme, and this design could quite easily be adapted for a round or square tray.

One of the great advantages of this project is that it can be made from collected scraps of white and colored paper. These have been cut and pasted onto a surface painted to provide a good color contrast to the starkness of the white paper. Once the finished tray has been painted with a number of coats of varnish, it becomes extremely durable and can be wiped down after use.

YOU WILL NEED

Blank tray with sloping sides
(this one is 11 × 17 in (28 × 43 cm)

Sheet of white cartridge paper
12 × 16 in (30 × 40 cm)

Scraps of recycled paper in tan,
orange, blue and turquoise

Templates (see page 185)

Paper clips and a fine black pen

Small pointed scissors and
pinking shears

Wallpaper paste (fungicide-free)

Acrylic varnish and brush

1 Fold the piece of the white paper in half across the width. Place the straight side of the plant template against the fold and hold in place with paper clips. Place the bird in the remaining space and draw around both templates with the black pen. Cut out carefully using the small scissors.

2 Cut out seven circles with a 1½ in (4 cm) diameter from the tan paper and another seven circles with a diameter of ¾ in (2 cm) from the yellow paper. Cut out two tan-colored wings.

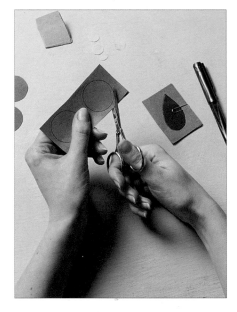

3 Open out the plant and, using the small scissors, snip out little V shapes all around the circular flowers. Take care not to cut too far in toward the center. Do exactly the same on the seven tan-colored circles.

4 Use the pinking shears to cut lengths of the white paper to form an internal border at the edge of the tray around the design. Cut some similar slightly narrower strips to fit around the upper rim of the tray.

5 Mix the wallpaper paste according to the packet instructions and lightly smear the inside edge of the tray and both sides of the paper strips. Lay the strips in position and smooth with the fingers to release any air bubbles. Next, paste down the plant in the same way (it is a good idea to measure the halfway point to help place the image centrally; the wallpaper paste allows you to manipulate the paper gently until it is correctly positioned).

The deep, sloping sides of this wooden tray make it ideal to use when serving breakfast in bed. Any accidental spills will be caught within the tray, thus protecting the bed linen. The pretty lace-edged napkin and freshly picked stem of flowering clematis help to create an elegant look.

6 Paste the tan circles over the white flowers and add the small yellow circles to the center. Stick the wing shapes in place on the bird and cut two yellow strips to decorate the wings. Cut a blue collar for the bird and decorate with a turquoise strip cut with pinking shears. Apply two similar strips to the pot.

7 Finally, paste the thinner strips around the rim of the tray. Allow to dry thoroughly overnight and give the tray at least three coats of acrylic varnish for protection, leaving the varnish to dry thoroughly between coats.

BEDSIDE POSY

AT THIS TIME OF YEAR there is relatively little flowering in the garden compared to the rich abundance of summer, and flower arrangements tend to be more modest. The advantage of this is that as each new type of flower opens, we can appreciate it all the more for its lack of rivals. Spring flowers usually have a delicacy of form and color that contribute to their early charm. Hellebores, pictured here, are a great favorite and appear in a range of subtle hues and faint patterns including green, purple and creamy white. They are combined in the pretty pink luster jug with the untidy blossoms of the fragrant *Clematis armandii*, one of the earliest evergreen climbers. As both types of flowers are long-lasting they make a very rewarding arrangement – a perfect touch when preparing a guest room.

EASTER BREAD

IN GREECE a special bread is made at Easter time that takes the form of a plait with real dyed eggs woven into the dough. The fresh egg is thus baked along with the bread. This is a lovely idea for a spring breakfast, with the egg symbolizing rebirth and the promise of new life.

Any bread recipe can be adapted for this project – here a simple focaccia has been used. The recipe below makes four loaves.

Edible egg dye in red or yellow
4 eggs
12 oz (350 g) all-purpose flour
½ tsp salt
2 tsp easy blend yeast
7½ fl oz (210 ml) warm water
1½ tbsp olive oil
Sea salt

Mix the egg dye according to the instructions and dye each egg evenly with color, then set the eggs aside.

Sift the flour and the salt into a bowl, add the yeast and mix together. Pour in the warm water and the oil and stir together until the mixture pulls away from the edge of the bowl. Turn out onto a floured surface and knead for about 10 minutes. Place back into the bowl, cover with a clean towel or plastic wrap and leave in a warm place to double in size – this takes about 1½ hours.

Turn the dough out again onto a floured surface and knead for a further 2 minutes. Divide into four and place on a greased baking tin. Using your fingers, make an egg-shaped hole in the center of each loaf and push an egg into each hole. Push the dough around the egg so it is securely in place. Sprinkle the top with sea salt and allow to rise for half an hour.

Preheat the oven to 375°F (190°C). Bake the loaves for 15–20 minutes or until the bread begins to turn golden.

CLOTH BREAD BASKET

THIS FABRIC BREAD BASKET makes an attractive container for serving freshly baked bread at breakfast time. The basket folds together with tapes tied into bows at each corner, holding the sides upright. The corner pleats can be folded either inside or outside the basket. Untied, it is easy to store flat when not in use. Ticking stripes in rich carthy colors add a utilitarian feel to the basket. The finished basket measures $12 \times 8\frac{1}{2} \times 3$ in ($30 \times 22 \times 7.5$ cm), but you could easily make this versatile container in a smaller version to hold biscuits or candies or with larger dimensions to keep socks and handkerchiefs in.

YOU WILL NEED

Piece of fabric 20 × 32 in (50 × 80 cm)

Pins

5½ feet (1.7 m) tape

Plastic board 18 × 14 in (45 × 36 cm)

Sewing thread and needle

Scissors

1 Cut two pieces of fabric each 19 × 15¾ in (48 × 40 cm). On one of the pieces draw lines with a pencil 4 in (10 cm) in from and parallel to all four sides to mark the stitching lines. Cut eight 8½ in (21 cm) lengths of tape and pin them 4 in (10 cm) in from each corner to the right side of one of the pieces and with one end level with the fabric edge.

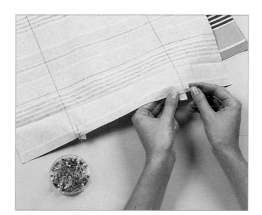

2 With right sides facing, pin the two pieces together and stitch along three sides (leaving one short end open). Trim the seams, turn to the right side and press. Turn under and press the seam allowance along the open end.

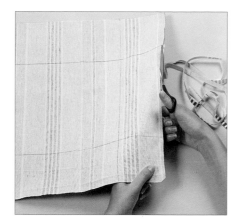

3 Cut rectangles of plastic board as follows: one base 11½ × 8½ in (29 × 21 cm), two sides 11½ × 2¾ in (29 × 7 cm) and two end pieces 8½ × 2¾ in (21 × 7 cm). Stitch a line 3 in (7.5 cm) in from and parallel to both long side edges to make two side channels and one channel in the center. Push one of the end pieces of board down the center channel until it meets the bottom end seam.

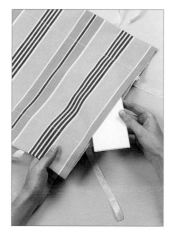

4 Using a zipper foot, stitch a line 3 in (7.5 cm) in from and parallel to the bottom edge to enclose the first piece of plastic board. Push the base board into the middle channel and the two side pieces of board down each side channel.

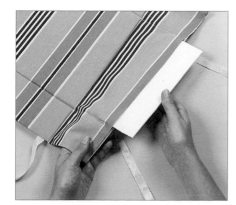

5 Stitch a line across the fabric 3 in (7.5 cm) in from and parallel to the open end to enclose the pieces of board. Push the last piece of board into the central channel.

6 Pin the open end together, then slip stitch to close it. Fold up the sides and tie the tapes to form a basket with a pleat at each corner.

Children's Easter Party

FINE SPRING DAYS with the warmth of sunshine in the air offer the first opportunity of the year for carrying the table and chairs out of doors. Take advantage of the good weather and make the garden the location for a children's tea party. They will appreciate the chance to run around, playing hide and seek among the trees and shrubs. Place the table under a tree in blossom to provide a gently dappled shade for the setting.

WOVEN
BASKETS

MOST PEOPLE TRY their hand weaving paper at some time. It is a fascinating yet easy to master technique and there is something almost magical about being able to make a strong and durable structure from strips of paper.

The pretty checked pattern shown here is created by weaving with different colored papers, and the rim has been sewn on using paper string, adding another decorative feature. Packed with a handful of colored straw, these baskets make an ideal container for a gift of Easter eggs — either real eggs or the miniature sugar-coated chocolate versions.

YOU WILL NEED

1 sheet of handmade
white paper, at least
7 × 13 in (18 × 33 cm)

1 smaller sheet each of pink,
brown and blue recycled paper

Small stapler and white glue

Clothespins

Scissors and pinking shears

Paper string

Long needle

1 Cut nine lengths of the white paper each 13 in
(33 cm) long and ¾ in (2 cm) wide. Lay five
lengths down in an even row and weave the other four
across them, leaving equidistant lengths all around.

2 When the strips
are neatly
woven together,
staple each corner
to hold the paper
firmly in place. This
helps to build up an
even shape when you
are weaving up the
four sides.

3 Cut four strips, two of pink and two of
brown ¾ in (2 cm) wide and 17 in
(43 cm) long. Bend up the remaining free
side strips so they are at right angles to the
base and start to weave the pink strip into
these uprights. To make the weaving more
secure, glue the strip behind a white upright
and finish off in the same way, hiding the
join on the inside of the basket.

4 Continue weaving alternate pink and
brown strips until there are two of each
in place. Glue at the beginning and end of
each strip. Take particular care when
weaving around the corners not to pull the
strips too tight and thus distort the form.

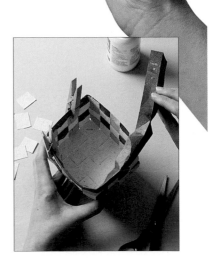

5 Dab some glue behind each white upright
and secure the top brown strip to the
uprights. Use the clothespins to hold the
strips in place
while the
glue sets.

6 Cut off the excess
white strips. Cut
a strip of the brown
paper 1½ × 16 in
(4 × 40 cm), fold in
half lengthways, dab
some glue into the fold
and place over the rim
of the basket. Hold in
place with the clothespins
while the glue sets.

7 Using the long needle, pierce a hole just below the brown rim in the top center of each of the pink and the white squares, through the two thicknesses of paper. Thread the paper string through the prepared holes and up and over the rim (you can do this without using the needle). When you have oversewn all around the rim, stick the end of the string inside the basket and cover the end with a matching square of paper.

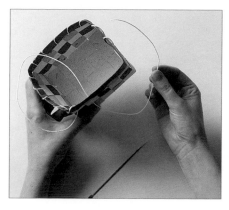

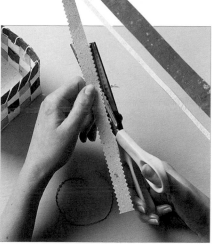

8 Cut a length of the brown paper 1¼ × 11 in (3 × 28 cm). Cut a strip of pink paper with the pinking shears ¾ × 11 in (2 × 28 cm) and a thinner strip of the white paper ¼ × 11 in (5 mm × 28 cm).

9 Using the white glue, stick the white strip onto the pink and the pink centrally onto the brown. Apply glue to the last 1¼ in (3 cm) of each end and stick in place behind the rim on the inside of the basket. Hold in place with two clothespins, one each side of the handle, until the glue dries.

CHOCOLATE EGGS WITH SUGAR VIOLETS

MOST PEOPLE would not think of making their own chocolate eggs but, as with many techniques, it is easy when you know how! You will need plastic egg molds and a piping bag – these are available from kitchen-supply stores. The violets are piped first onto paper and allowed to set hard to make them easier to handle. It is well worth making your own sugar flowers as they can be expensive to buy.

As you become more proficient at casting chocolate you can make larger eggs and even pipe the names of friends and family on them in decorative lettering. This quantity of chocolate will make about three eggs, each the size of a hen's egg.

YOU WILL NEED

9 oz (250 g) good quality
dark chocolate

Plastic mold, two parts for six
eggs or one part for three

Heatproof bowl and small
saucepan, to make a bain-marie

Spoon and knife

Baking parchment

Cotton gloves (see step 3)

Kitchen paper

Piping bag and decorative nozzle

Royal icing, tinted with violet
food coloring

1 To melt the chocolate, break the bars into small pieces and place in a bain-marie over a low heat. When the chocolate is fluid, remove the pan from the heat and pour a spoonful into each half-mold. Angle the mold so the chocolate spreads evenly up to the edges. Leave the mold in a cold place to set, then add two more layers in the same way. Allow the chocolate to set hard.

2 To release the egg shape, hold the mold upside down over a sheet of baking parchment and press gently but firmly onto the back of the mold. This will allow the egg to come out.

3 Put on the cotton gloves — these will help to prevent marking the eggs when handling them. Stick the two halves of the egg together by spreading a little melted chocolate onto the rim of each side to act as glue. Press the two halves together, rest on a folded paper towel and leave in a cold place until completely set.

4 Scrape off any excess chocolate around the join with a knife. Put the royal icing into the piping bag and attach the nozzle for a narrow flattened line. Holding the egg gently in one hand, pipe a wavy line of icing around the join. Put the egg aside and allow the icing to set hard.

5 Attach a petal nozzle to the icing bag and pipe the violets onto a sheet of baking parchment. First, pipe a large wavy single petal at the top, then follow with two separate petals below. Allow to set hard. (Piping sets are often supplied with useful instructions showing how to use the different nozzles.)

6 Holding the egg carefully in one hand, pipe a drop of icing onto the middle of one side to serve as glue and press the violet into place. Store in a cool place until ready to eat.

EASTER BONNET

CHILDREN LOVE TO DRESS UP and Easter provides the perfect occasion. Easter bonnets can be as wild as you please, decorated with ribbons, bows and a herbaceous border of real or fake flowers. Embellish an old straw hat or make a simple cardboard bonnet embellished with whatever is at hand to create a milliner's delight. The finished article does not have to last forever, so take shortcuts and glue buttons to the crown, trim with bits of braid and finish with a lavish length of taffeta ribbon.

YOU WILL NEED

Stiff corrugated paperboard, about 16½ × 11¾ in (42 × 30 cm)

Template (see page 184)

Scissors

Bradawl

Cord

Tissue paper

Double-sided tape and glue

Oddments of braid

1⅓ yards (1.3 m) taffeta ribbon, 1½ in (4 cm) wide

Needle and thread

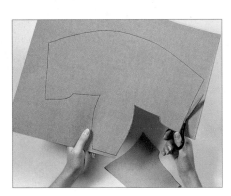

1 Draw the crown shape onto the paper-board using the template, then cut it out. You can change the size of the template to fit the child's head, if you wish.

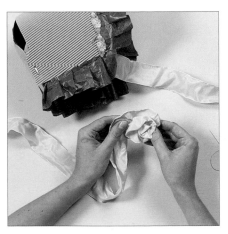

2 Bend down the sides to meet the back and make pairs of holes on each side with a bradawl where indicated on the template. Thread short lengths of cord through the corresponding sets of holes and tie together on the inside. Trim the ends.

3 Cut strips of tissue paper 2½ in (6 cm) deep and pleat them to make two lengths to fit across the front and base of the crown. Stick them in place with double-sided tape. Decorate the bonnet as required with bits of braid glued in place.

4 Cut the taffeta ribbon into two lengths. Make a ribbon rose at one end of each by folding the end of the ribbon lengthways then, keeping the selvages underneath the flower, pleat and turn the ribbon around itself a few times to form the center. Secure at the base with a few stitches. Begin to open out the ribbon and continue pleating, turning and stitching it at the base as the rose forms. Cut a slit close to the corner of the bonnet on each side and thread the ribbon through so that the rose is on the front.

STENCILED TABLECLOTH

SETTING THE TABLE for a special occasion is well worth the extra effort, and you can be spurred on by knowing that your creativity is contributing to a memorable event. Stenciling is an easy way to decorate table linen and stunning results can be achieved in a very short time. Here we have taken charming ceramic rabbits discovered in a thrift shop as the starting point for the design, copying their chunky rounded shapes to make the stencil. You can work as many or as few of the motifs on the cloth as you like, then finish each one with a bow stitched around the neck. If you wish, you can simply stencil the design onto a ready-made cloth. The finished cloth shown here measures 44 in (112 cm) square.

YOU WILL NEED

1⅓ yds (1.3 m) linen,
60 in (150 cm) wide

Sewing thread and pins

Scissors

Stencil paper

Craft knife and cutting mat

Spray glue and masking tape

Scrap paper

Fabric paints and stencil brushes

Kitchen towel

1 yard (1 m) ribbon,
½ in (1 cm) wide

5½ yards (5 m) ribbon,
1½ in (4 cm) wide

1 Cut a square of linen 50 × 50 in (125 × 125 cm). Make hems on all four sides, turning under ¾ in (1.5 cm), then 2 in (5 cm) to the wrong side, pin and press. Miter the corners for a flat, professional finish. Pin, then stitch the hem in place.

2 Make a guideline to mark the position of the stenciling and ribbon border by working lines of long tacking stitches 7 in (18 cm) from and parallel to the hemmed edges of the cloth.

4 Place the stencil centrally on the guideline, with the line running along the base of the design. Mask off the grass at the sides of the design with scrap paper and tape. Load the brush with paint, dab the brush on kitchen paper until it is almost dry, then brush over the rabbit shape, applying the color lightly. Mask the rabbit and stencil the grass in the same way. Carefully remove the stencil. Repeat on the remaining sides of the tablecloth.

3 Draw the design onto stencil paper following the template on page 186. Cut out the stencil using a craft knife and cutting mat. Mark the center point of each guideline with a few tacking stitches. Apply a coat of spray glue to the back of the stencil.

5 Dry iron the painted areas on the wrong side of the cloth to fix. Tie four bows in narrow ribbon and stitch one at the neck of each rabbit. Pin the wide ribbon around the cloth, matching the inside edge to the guideline and turning corners. Stitch in place.

Table Settings

RIGHT: *A simple rabbit shape cut from manila paper makes a decorative tag when fastened with a length of satin ribbon to the handle of a child's painted wicker basket. Other beastly caricatures such as chickens, bears or snails would work just as well. An Easter basket can be filled with all sorts of special treats to make the seasonal celebration memorable.*

ABOVE: *Fancy ribbon decorated with Easter chicks and daisies is used to tie up napkins in keeping with the theme of the table, making a pretty feature at each place setting.*

LEFT: *Pottery rabbits are used to decorate the Easter table and reinforce the seasonal theme.*

ABOVE: *Miniature tin buckets are filled with delicious Easter eggs and included in the annual egg hunt that sends the children scouting around the garden in search of edible treats. These colorful containers look lovely hanging among the apple blossoms.*

RIGHT: *Chocolate Easter boxes filled with speckled sugar-coated eggs and tied with ribbon look like miniature parcels. Milk chocolate thins are used like tiles to form the box sides. To make them, cut a square of cardboard the same size as the chocolate thins to form the base and lay a length of thin ribbon under the cardboard. Cut sponge cake into cubes slightly smaller than the chocolate squares and place one on each cardboard base. Coat the cake's sides and top with chocolate butter icing and stick a chocolate tile to each side. Arrange a few eggs on the top, pushing them into the icing, and add a tilting chocolate square as the lid. Tie the ribbon around the box in a bow and trim the ends.*

ABOVE: *Checked handkerchiefs make little goody bags when tied to the ends of sticks, so children can leave the party with their belongings carried on their shoulders. Each bag holds a lollipop, some foil-wrapped chocolate eggs and a tiny gift. Lay the handkerchiefs flat and place the gifts in the middle, gather up the four corners together to contain them, then tie to the stick ends with lengths of ribbon.*

LEAF-STENCILED EGGS

IN MANY PARTS OF THE WORLD, Easter is a time for giving eggs, most often in the form of confectionery or chocolate, but the old tradition of decorating real eggs is still alive. The egg is a perfect form and lends itself to decoration using many different techniques that are a delight to make with family and friends. Here they have been stenciled and dyed for a dramatic effect.

Instructions for the tartan eggs, made with strips of contrasting colored paper cut with scissors or pinking shears and pasted around the shells to resemble a tartan pattern, are given overleaf.

If you wish to keep the eggs, blow them before decorating. Do this by piercing a small hole at each end of the egg and draining the contents.

YOU WILL NEED

Small leaves, freshly picked

Old pair of panty hose

Small scissors

Old stainless steel pan

Natural dyes, such as logwood, redwood and yellow wood

Plate

Pile white duck eggs in a pretty china bowl and display with other white objects.

1 Wet the surface of the egg and carefully lay the leaf centrally in place on the egg, gently smoothing out any folds or wrinkles in the leaf.

2 Cut the panty hose into 6 in (15 cm) lengths. Wrap a length around the egg, pulling tightly to hold the leaf in place. Tie the tights into a knot at the back.

3 In an old pan, bring the dye to a boil and allow to cool slightly before lowering the egg in. Simmer gently for about 10 minutes or until the required depth of color is achieved.

4 Lift the eggs out of the pan, hold briefly under running water to cool and then rest them on a plate. Snip the knot in the panty hose open, pull the fabric away from the egg and gently peel off the leaf to reveal the undyed shell beneath.

PAPER-DECORATED EGGS

THERE ARE COUNTLESS WAYS of decorating eggs. This country craft has a long tradition and exquisite examples exist of painted, engraved, dyed, batiked, gilded and decoupaged eggs, particularly in Europe. These tartan strip eggs are easy to make and, although papercutting is a traditional technique, the design on these eggs has a contemporary feel. The decoration is added to blown eggs (see previous spread) so they can be kept and displayed indefinitely.

YOU WILL NEED

Large blown eggs

Scraps of colored paper in pink, purple and brown

Scissors

Pinking shears

Wallpaper paste (fungicide-free)

Small bowl for mixing paste

Acrylic varnish and brush

1 Cut two lengths of pink paper roughly ½ in (1 cm) wide and long enough to reach around the egg lengthways with a small overlap. Cut three similar strips of the purple paper two to reach around lengthways and one to go around the width of the egg. Cut four long strips of brown paper ¼ in (5 mm) wide and use the pinking shears to add a decorative edge to one side.

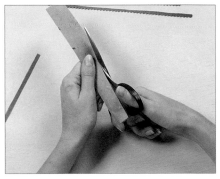

2 Mix up the wallpaper paste and smear it evenly onto both sides of the pink strips and also onto the surface of the egg. Stick the two strips in place, dividing the egg into quarters.

3 Apply the purple strips in the same manner, placing them equidistantly between the pink strips, and with one strip around the center of the egg.

4 Now apply the brown pinked strips, placing the straight edges against the purple strips and leaving a ⅛ in (3 mm) margin of shell showing between the colors. Allow to dry thoroughly, then apply a coat of acrylic varnish for protection.

DISPLAYING EGGS

ABOVE: *Sometimes simplicity is all. Hard-boil the eggs, adding an Easter egg dye to the boiling water to turn them a single color, and find an unusual way to display them. This curious little hen-shaped basket comes from Madeira and makes an ideal container for the breakfast table at Easter time.*

LEFT: *Treasures of the traditional Easter egg hunt are usually of the delicious, glittering chocolate variety. For a more unusual idea, place small pheasants' eggs in a real bird's nest and hide it in the garden among silvery leaves for children to find for breakfast on Easter morning.*

ABOVE: *Although it is very rewarding to decorate eggs, their natural colors and shapes have an exquisite beauty that cannot be surpassed. Pile a quantity of pure white duck eggs into a pretty white china stemmed bowl and display on a windowsill with other white objects to make a serene "still life" arrangement.*

Spring Lunch

A FINE SPRING DAY offers an opportunity to open the windows and allow the outside in. These rays of sunshine early in the year are a welcome and cheering sight. For a special spring lunch, choose a color combination that reflects the freshness of the world outside, such as classic blue and cream. Flowers that are in season, such as bluebells and hyacinths, come in deep inky-blue shades that look stunning alongside pure white snowdrops, paperwhites and crocuses. Use colored china and glassware to enhance this mood.

CROSS-STITCHED NAPKINS

C ROSS-STITCH is one of the easiest embroidery stitches to master. Worked over an even grid of squares formed by the fabric background, patterns and motifs quickly form. Here, inspired by blue and white china, a simple flower in the china design has been interpreted in stitches to make a set of napkins echoing the style of the plates.

Linen fabric with an even-weave construction is commonly used for cross-stitch embroidery as the threads are easy to count to keep the stitches uniform, but here waffle cotton, which has a grid of squares to make plotting the design really easy, has been chosen.

1 Cut out a 21 in (53 cm) square in waffle cotton for each napkin. Press under ½ in (1 cm) on all four sides, then a further ¾ in (2 cm) turning to make the hems. Pin the hems in place, making mitered corners where the hems meet. Stitch the hems in place close to the turning and secure the mitered corners with a few slip stitches.

2 Mark out the position of the motif on one corner of the napkin, evenly placed within the two hemmed edges, by counting the squares on the fabric to correspond to the squares on the chart, marking the corner points with pins then with tacking stitches. Work two more lines of tacking to cross at the center of the motif area.

YOU WILL NEED

1¼ yds (1.1 m) waffle cotton, 54 in (137 cm) wide – this makes four napkins, each 18½ in (47 cm) square

Scissors

Pins

Sewing thread

Motif chart (see page 184)

5 skeins of stranded cotton embroidery thread

Embroidery needle

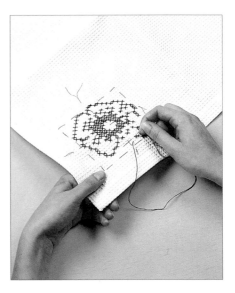

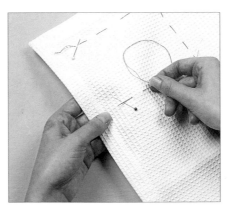

3 Work the motif in cross-stitch, using three strands of embroidery thread throughout and making a stitch on the fabric to correspond with each square marked on the chart. When the stitching is complete, remove the tacking. If you wish, work a continuous row of cross-stitches all around the napkin just within the hemmed area and an even distance from each edge to complete.

CHINA SHARD NAPKIN TIE

SOME PEOPLE find it hard to throw away broken china, especially if the pieces are from a favorite or valuable antique plate. These unusual little medallions have been made by embedding each shard into a polymer clay surround. This not only protects against the sharp edges but makes it possible to insert a wire loop at the top. Attach a medallion to each end of a length of matching cross-grained ribbon to make a napkin tie to coordinate with the china.

YOU WILL NEED

Shards of blue and white china

Tile nippers, goggles and mask (optional)

Short length of galvanized wire, 1/16 in (1 mm) thick

Resin glue

1 block of white polymer clay

24 in (60 cm) blue cross-grained ribbon, 1¼ in (3 cm) wide

Needle and thread

1 *If necessary, trim the edges of the china shard into a suitable shape with the tile nippers. (You should wear goggles and a mask while doing this.) Make a loop in a small length of wire and stick at the top of the china using the resin glue. Allow to set.*

2 *Cut a line of the clay from the block and work it between your fingers until it is soft. Mold the roll of clay around the sharp edges of the shard, covering the ends of the wire loop. Neaten the join and bake the medallion in the oven according to the packet instruction to set the clay.*

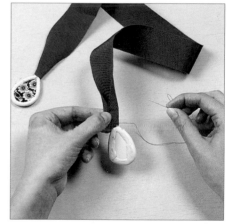

3 *Fold under a small hem on the ribbon and wrap around the wire loop at the top of the medallion. Wrap both sides to the back of the loop and sew tightly in place.*

SUMMER

A Day at the Beach

T HERE IS SOMETHING so enjoyable about a day at the beach. The light has an exquisite quality with vistas reaching to infinity and sea breezes seem able to blow cares and worries away. Whether wandering over sand dunes, beachcombing for treasures or splashing about in rockpools, it provides the ultimate in relaxation. Children especially love vacations by the sea. Building castles and exotic labyrinths in the sand, running freely along the beach and paddling at the water's edge are what make these days particularly carefree and memorable.

Finding a good spot on the beach to set up camp calls for all hands on deck, with the willing and not so willing helping to carry all the paraphernalia needed for a special day.

BEACH CANOPY

YOU WILL NEED

8 yds (7.5 m) of 72 in (183 cm)
wide canvas

Tape measure

Scissors

Pins

⅝ in (12 mm) eyelets and tool

Wooden board

4 flat washers

34 yds (31 m) nylon cord

10 guy rope guides

10 long tent pegs

12 yds (11 m) cotton tape,
½ in (1 cm) wide

12½ yds (11.6 m) cotton tape,
1 in (2.5 cm) wide

4 yds (3.6 m) Velcro

Sewing thread

Heavy duty machine needle

1 in (4×28 mm) wide wooden dowel
poles, each 7 ft 6 in (1.95 m) long

Saw

4 wooden door handles with screw
fittings (for the finials)

FOR LAZY DAYS at the sea, a beach hut is a much sought-after item, providing a home from home and a base for beach paraphernalia. A beach tent comes a close second and has the added advantage of being transportable.

Constructed over four poles that form the corner posts and are held in place with guy ropes and tent pegs, this canopy makes the perfect setting for a beach barbecue. The tent sides can be attached when needed, to be rolled down for extra shade during the hottest time of the day as well as making a windbreak on a breezy beach. It also provides privacy for changing into bathing suits or a shady corner for an afternoon nap.

The same idea could be adapted to make a garden canopy to shade a bench or, lit with lanterns, for an evening dinner party.

The finished canopy measures approximately 5 ft 10 in (180 cm) wide and deep.

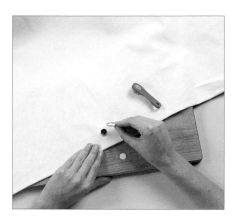

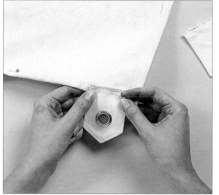

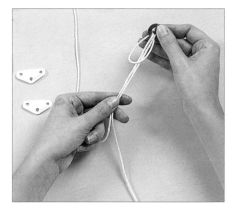

1 For the main part of the canopy, cut a length of canvas 72 in (183 cm) wide by 143 in (363 cm) long. Turn and pin under ⅜ in (15 mm) hems to the wrong side along all four edges and stitch along both long hems and one short one. Using pins on the side hems, mark fold lines across the width of the fabric, the first 59 in (150 cm) in from the back hemmed edge and the other 12 in (30 cm) in from the front pinned edge. Make eyelets at each of these pin marks 1½ in (4 cm) in from the sides, following the packet instructions.

2 Make two flaps by cutting out four pieces of canvas 4 × 3¼ in (10 × 8 cm). Take two of these pieces and, with right sides facing, stitch along both long sides and one short side, shaping the short edge into a V shape and taking ½ in (1 cm) seams. Trim seams, turn to right side and press. Top-stitch ¼ in (5 mm) in from the edges on the three turned sides. Make the second flap in the same way. Insert an eyelet on each flap, placed centrally but toward the pointed edge. Place the raw edge of each flap underneath the pinned hem of the canopy, ¾ in (2 cm) in from the side edges and stitch the hem.

3 Cut four lengths of cord 6⅔ yds (6.2 m) long and two lengths 3⅓ yds (3.1 m) long. Thread a guy rope guide through both ends of each long length of cord and knot to secure. Fix a guy rope guide to one end of both of the shorter lengths of cord in the same way. Fold a long length in half to make a loop and thread it through a flat washer, threading the rest of the cord through the loop to secure. Attach the other three long lengths to flat washers in the same way.

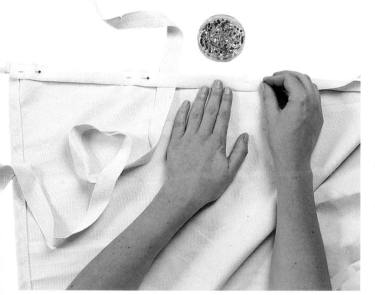

4 For the sides, cut out two canvas pieces 72 in (183 cm) square. To slope the top edge, make a mark 12 in (30 cm) down from one edge and draw a line from this point to the corresponding corner on both pieces and cut along the line. Turn under hems on the three straight edges and stitch, making the second side the reverse of the first. Turn under the hem on the sloping edge and pin.

Cut the wide cotton tape into four equal lengths. Lay two pieces centrally over the pinned hem, 16 in (40 cm) in from the side edges. Pin a length of Velcro over the hem and tape, then stitch through all the layers. Finish the second side in the same way.

To make the side ties for when the sides are down, cut twelve 24 in (60 cm) lengths of narrow cotton tape. Fold each length in half to find the center point and stitch the center point to the side hems, three down each side and evenly spaced. Stitch lengths of Velcro between the eyelets along the side hems on the top of the canopy so the canopy sides can be attached when needed.

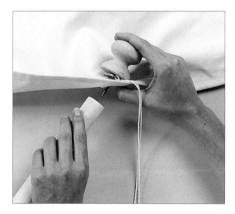

5 Use two poles 7 ft 6 in (1.95 m) long for the canopy front. Cut the other two poles to a length of 5 ft 5 in (1.65 m) for the back. (This allows 6 in [15 cm] at the base of each pole to push into the sand.) Hold a front pole top below one of the front eyelets, place a flat washer with cord attached over the eyelet and screw the door handle into the pole from the top to secure. Attach the other poles and cords in the same way. Tie the raw ends of the shorter cord lengths to the front flaps. Cut six 24 in (60 cm) lengths of thin tape and stitch them centrally, three equally spaced on each side, to the canopy back side hems for rolling up the back.

SHELL MIRROR FRAME

DECORATING WITH ASSORTED SHELLS is a traditional craft much favored during the nineteenth century. Extravagant examples of this art can be found in romantic grottoes decorated from floor to ceiling with thousands of shells and in the beautiful pictures often made by sailors with exotic shells found on their travels. Most projects, however, were created on a more modest scale, such as frames, small boxes and brooches.

The mirror frame shown here is decorated with a basic structure of small white scallop shells and filled in with assorted pale-colored shells to make a border and to hide any gaps. This is a wonderful way of preserving and displaying a treasured collection.

YOU WILL NEED

Blank wooden frame – the one used here is approximately 7 × 8¾ in (18 × 22 cm) with surround 2 in (5 cm) wide

Small kitchen knife

Tub of tile-and-grout adhesive

1 large scallop shell

9 small scallop shells

Collection of mixed shells including some small conical shapes

Brush

Jam jar, for water

Paper towels

1 Using the knife, liberally spread some of the adhesive along the top section of the frame and stick the large shell in the center. Place a smaller scallop shell on each side, covering the corners of the frame. The shells should overlap the outside edge, leaving space along the inside edge for adding smaller shells.

2 Using the collection of smaller shells, create a symmetrical design on either side of the large central shell, pushing them firmly into the adhesive.

3 Spread the adhesive down each side of the frame and add three more shells beneath the corner ones. Make sure that the base corner shell overlaps the side and base of the frame by the same amount as the top row of shells.

4 Push the conical shells into the spaces between the scallops. Work on both sides of the frame simultaneously, making a symmetrical design. Fill in the remaining space using a selection of the smaller shells. Complete the bottom of the frame in the same way.

5 Allow the adhesive to begin to harden a little – this should take about ten minutes. Wash the brush in water and wipe on a piece of paper towel to remove excess water which may weaken the setting adhesive. Then carefully clean off any unwanted white adhesive from the shells.

Beachcombing

LEFT: *Large specimen shells with their subtle shades of pink, purple and pearly luster make beautiful arrangements in the bathroom. Their structure is endlessly fascinating and one can easily serve as a soap dish. Use your favorite shell as a starting point for choosing the color scheme for your bathroom. Even towels, soap and bath mat can reflect and complement the natural form and color.*

ABOVE: *Strong gusts of wind are often a problem near the sea, so here is a clever idea for weighting down a tablecloth at a beach picnic. Metal eyelets have been punched around the edge of a brightly printed oilcloth. Use raffia to tie a collection of larger pierced shells and stones through the holes.*

ABOVE: *Endless hours can be spent beachcombing at the seaside. Simple finds take on great significance and are often transformed into treasures. Particularly prized are stones with holes worn through them. On this flotsam and jetsam wreath they have been tied with shells, feathers, seaweed and driftwood to make a lasting memento of a happy summer vacation.*

LEFT: *Few people can resist picking up an unusual stone on the beach, but the skill is in finding interesting ways of displaying it at home. This collection of bleached white, elongated stones have been arranged in a circle on a garden table and can remain outside all year.*

SAILBOATS

CHILDREN ARE ALWAYS FASCINATED with boats and floating items found on the beach or in rockpools at the seaside. Shells, feathers, dried seaweed and driftwood can provide endless interest. These little sailboats, however, have been made at home using little boat-shaped tartlet cases (barquettes) with a wire mast. If you can find them, it is best to use the aluminum variety, which float more easily. Add a different colored sail to each one and you are all set for a seaside regatta.

YOU WILL NEED

Length of galvanized wire 1/16 in (1.5 mm) thick

Wire cutters

Pliers

Quick-setting resin glue

Boat-shaped tartlet molds, 11 cm (4½ in) long and 2 cm (¾ in) or more deep

Blue and white metal paint

Paintbrush

Waxed or plasticized paper in a choice of colors

Small hole punch

Scissors

1 Cut a length of wire 4¾ in (12 cm) long. Use the pliers to twist the end into a tight, flat coil. Bend the coil at right angles to the remaining length of wire and use the glue to stick this mast centrally into the base of the boat. Allow the glue to set.

2 Paint the inside of the boat and the mast white, allow to dry thoroughly and then paint the outside of the boat blue.

3 Cut little triangles from the paper with right-angled sides that measure 3¼ and 2½ in (8 and 6 cm). Punch four holes along the 3¼ in (8 cm) side and thread the mast through these holes on alternate sides to hold it firmly in place.

SEASIDE PINWHEEL

A DAY AT THE BEACH JUST wouldn't be the same without the traditional pinwheel stuck into the soft sand, buzzing around and showing the direction the wind is blowing from. This is an enduring children's toy that has scarcely changed in design over the years, its marvelously simple construction playfully demonstrating the force and energy of the wind.

It is best to make them out of plastic or plastic-covered paper so they can handle rain and sea spray without becoming damaged. Once you have mastered the technique, make a number to mark your spot on the sand.

YOU WILL NEED

Chromatica paper (thick, colored
tracing paper), one sheet in yellow
and one in blue

Template (see page 184)

Pen

Scissors

Hole punch, ¼ in (5 mm) size

Eyelet kit, ¼ in (5 mm) size

Hammer

Wooden board

20 in (50 cm) length of dowel,
½ in (1 cm) thick

Gimlet

6 in (15 cm) length of galvanized
wire, ¹⁄₁₆ in (1.6 mm) thick

Plastic drinking straw or
fine plastic tubing

Pliers

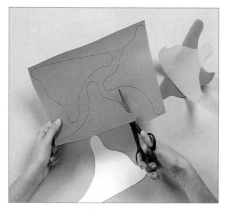

1 Lay the template on the colored paper, draw around the shape with the pen and cut out with the scissors. You will need to cut four sails from each of the two colors.

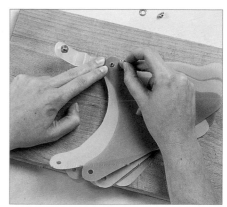

2 Make a pile of alternate colors from the individual sails. Punch holes through the two longer ends (the hole punch will punch two or three thicknesses at a time). Following the instructions on the eyelet kit, fix all the shorter ends together.

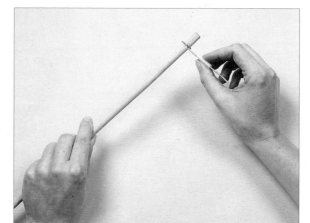

3 Make a hole right through the dowel ¾ in (2 cm) from one end using the gimlet. Thread the wire through the hole and wrap around the dowel once to secure tightly. Cut a ¾ in (2 cm) length from the plastic straw and thread onto the projecting wire.

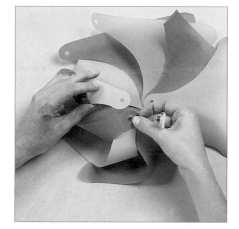

4 Open out the pinwheel sails evenly and bring each one forward individually to overlap the one beneath. Place the eyelet tool underneath with the eyelets in place, according to the instructions. Bend the tool over and bang firmly with the hammer to secure the eyelet in position.

5 Thread the opened-out sail onto the wire with the eyelet join facing outward. Use the pliers to bend over the remaining section of wire into securing loop.

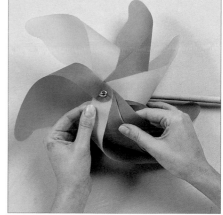

6 Finally, carefully pull each individual sail to make it equidistant from the next. When they are all evenly spaced, the pinwheel should spin smoothly.

CANVAS BEACH BAG

E VERYONE NEEDS a roomy beach bag for carting all the necessary paraphernalia to the beach. A roomy carryall will hold towels, swimming gear and a picnic lunch down to the sea shore with enough room left to bring back the prized pebbles and shells collected from a busy day's beachcombing.

Canvas is a material traditionally used on boats so it perfectly captures the feel of the seaside and makes a bag that is extremely hardwearing. Look for treated canvas with a showerproof surface for the most durable finish, and choose the heaviest weight that can be sewn on a domestic sewing machine (you may need to buy a sturdier needle for your machine). Natural rope bought from a yacht chandler makes simple knotted handles for a finishing touch with a nautical feel.

YOU WILL NEED

1⅔ yds (1.5 m) canvas, 36 in (90 cm) wide

Pattern paper

Pen or pencil

Templates (see page 187)

Scissors

Sewing thread

Bias binding

⅜ in (12 mm) eyelet kit

1¼ yds (1.1 m) rope, ⅜ in (12 mm) thick

1 Draw the pattern pieces on paper copying the templates (a ¾ in [15 mm] seam allowance is included throughout). Cut out the pieces in canvas as follows: two side pieces, two top borders, two bottom borders and one base. Fold under the seam allowance along the bottom edges of both top borders, clip curves and press. With right side of the top border to the wrong side of the side piece, pin borders to the side pieces and stitch along top edges. Trim seams and clip curves, then turn each border to the right side and pin in place on the side piece along the folded edge. Press, then top-stitch close to the fold.

2 Fold under the seam allowance along the top edges of both bottom borders, clip curves and press. With the wrong side of bottom borders facing the right side of the side pieces, pin in place on the side pieces, matching bottom and side edges. Top-stitch close to the border fold, then tack along the other three sides to hold the layers together.

3 With right sides facing, pin both side pieces together and stitch down the side seams. With right sides facing, pin the base into the bag and stitch in place. Bind all the raw seams with bias binding to prevent them fraying. Turn the bag to the right side.

4 Following the instructions on the packet, make a pair of eyelets centrally placed on each side of the bag 1½ in (4 cm) down from the top and 6¾ in (17 cm) apart. Cut the rope in half. Thread each length through one pair of eyelets, adjusting the lengths to make handles the required size, then knot and fray the ends to fix them in place on the outside of the bag.

Picnic on the Beach

RIGHT: *Serving hot food at the beach calls for a fair amount of organization. Supermarkets sell small disposable barbecues suitable for just one use that are ideal. A small bucket barbecue that can be used throughout the summer is a more durable alternative, becoming a carrier for essentials such as charcoal and skewers on the way to the beach as well as a container for later taking away the resulting garbage. Keep the food simple but delicious for a memorable day, and don't forget to take some matches!*

ABOVE: *Sand in the sandwiches has become part of our treasured childhood memories of traditional summer days by the sea. Keeping sandwiches well wrapped or boxed will help them stay fresh and sand-free. Use waxed paper to wrap them, then tie the folded bundles with natural raffia and add a shell for an extra decorative flourish.*

LEFT: *For the beach, choose frosted plastic or glass tumblers that capture the look of weathered glass nuggets washed ashore on the tide. Beachcombing is an essential part of relaxing days by the sea, and it is impossible to resist the temptation to fill pockets with flotsam and jetsam, shells and pebbles.*

BELOW: *Illuminate an evening beach party or barbecue with votive candles in old jam jars. Twisted wire, wound around the top of the jar and threaded through a worn pebble found on the beach, can be used to decorate the handles. Take the jar home to hang in the garden or decorate the mantel.*

ABOVE: *Ruby red sorrel drink is a favorite beverage in the Caribbean and has an exquisite flavor unlike anything else. It is traditionally made from sorrel flowers, which are a type of hibiscus (Hibiscus sabdrifa). When fresh flowers are unavailable it can be made using the dried flowers. It is easy to make but needs to be prepared the night before it is needed. Pour into small plastic bottles that are easy to transport and store them with frozen ice packs to keep chilled for a welcome sunshine drink.*

Boil 4½ pints (2.5 liters) water. Place 4¾ oz (140 g) dried sorrel, ½ oz (15 g) fresh peeled ginger, ½ teaspoon whole cloves, 1 cinnamon stick broken into pieces, a few strips of orange and lemon and lime peel in a large pan or bowl and pour the water over. Stir and leave to steep overnight. Strain off the liquid and sweeten to taste with sugar. Bottle and store in the fridge until needed.

LEFT: *Seashells with naturally worn holes through them are useful finds on the beach. Use them to decorate makeshift napkin rings. Just thread cord through the holes and tie them loosely.*

Alfresco Eating

OUTDOOR EATING is one of the joys of summer. When the sun shines, what can be better than relaxing in the garden with friends and family. Placing the table close to the house has the advantage that it is not too far to transport the tableware, making it easier to create a stunning setting in an uncomplicated way. Choose delicately colored glassware to glint in the sunlight alongside bowls of luscious summer fruits. Finish off the table with handfuls of fresh summer blooms, gathered and bunched together in a simple container to capture the abundance of the season.

FLORAL SEAT COVERS

DRESS UP OLD garden chairs in these neatly scalloped fabric covers and bring an instant elegance to alfresco summer lunches. Choose a fabric to complement the colors in your garden or conservatory – here a floral print in green and white sits comfortably in a sunny corner.

Making the seat cover pattern

The seat cover is made to fit over an existing cushion. Alternatively, cut a piece of 1½ in (4 cm) thick foam to cover the seat. Lay the cushion on pattern paper and draw around it, mark the center points on each side and add ⅝ in (1.5 cm) seam allowance all around.

Measure the front of the cushion between both front corners. Draw a rectangle with this measurement for the long sides and 4½ in (12 cm) deep. Add ⅝ in (1.5 cm) seam allowance to all sides and mark the center front. Fold the rectangle in half along the center marking, then fold again bringing the center fold to meet the seam allowance line. Draw a curve from one edge of the center fold to 1⅜ in (3.5 cm) along the quarter fold. Cut through all thicknesses of paper following the curved line to make the wavy edge on the skirt.

Measure one side of cushion between front and back corners and make a pattern for the skirt sides in the same way. Measure the back of the cushion between the chair back bars and make a pattern for the skirt back in the same way, so it will fall between the back bars when complete.

Making the seat top pattern

Measure along the top edge of the seat back and add an extra ½ in (1 cm) for ease. Draw a rectangle on pattern paper 8 in (20 cm) deep and the top seat measurement wide. Add ⅝ in (1.5 cm) seam allowance to each side and mark the center point. Fold the paper into four as for the skirt side pattern, draw a curve and cut in the same way to make a wavy edge. When cutting out the lining, fold under the top edge seam allowance and place this edge against a fold so that the lining will be a single piece of fabric.

Allow extra fabric as required for pattern matching and cut pattern pieces as follows:
Seat: cut one in main fabric, one in lining
Skirt front: cut two in main fabric
Skirt back: cut two in main fabric
Skirt sides: cut four in main fabric
Seat top: cut two in main fabric
Seat top lining: cut one in lining

YOU WILL NEED

1¼ yds (1 m) lining fabric,
54 in (137 cm) wide

¾ yd (50 cm) calico,
48 in (120 cm) wide

4¼ yds (3.7 m) cotton tape
1 in (25 mm) wide

Pattern paper

Needle and thread

Scissors

Pins

Sewing machine

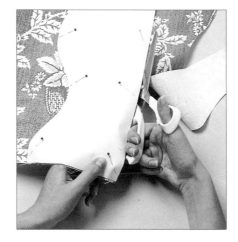

1 Cut out the pattern as instructed and pin to the fabric, matching and placing patterns centrally wherever necessary, then carefully cut the fabric pieces out.

2 Press under the seam allowance on the long straight edge of the skirt front. With right sides together, pin both skirt front pieces together and stitch down the sides and along the wavy edge. Trim the seam allowance to ¼ in (5 mm).

3 Snip the curved edge of the seam allowance at ¼ in (2 cm) intervals. Turn skirt front to the right side and press. Make the side and back skirt pieces in the same way as the front skirt.

4 Place the seat main fabric on the lining and stay-stitch them together ½ in (1 cm) in from all edges. Snip the corners to the stay-stitching and back edge of the seat where the back skirt will end within the back bars. With wrong sides together, pin the skirt front to the seat front and stitch together. Trim the seam, press the skirt to the right side and pin the folded edge to enclose the seam. Top-stitch close to the fold. Join the other skirt pieces to the seat in the same way.

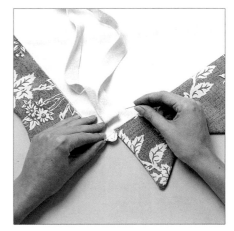

5 Fold under the tabs of fabric on either side of the back skirt to the wrong side and slip-stitch in place. To make the seat ties, cut two tapes 33 in (85 cm) long, fold them in half and stitch in place over the slip-stitched tabs. Neaten the tape ends if necessary. Place the cover onto the chair and slip-stitch the front skirt edges together to a depth of 2¼ in (6 cm).

6 To make the seat top, with right sides together, pin and stitch the two seat top pieces along the top edge. Press the seam open. With right sides together, pin the seat top and lining together and stitch all around, leaving a 4 in (10 cm) opening on one side edge. Trim the seam and turn to the right side. Turn under the edges of the opening,

pin and slip-stitch closed, then press. Cut four tapes each 18 in (45 cm) long and stitch them in place on the lining, positioned so they will sit within the back bars of the chair. Neaten the tape ends if necessary. Place the seat top over the chair back and slip-stitch the sides together to a depth of 4 in (10 cm).

ORGANDY CLOTH

T HE CRISP AND translucent nature of organdy makes it the perfect material for summer table linen. It looks quite beautiful when caught by a gentle breeze when the table is set outdoors and stunning when dressed with glass plates and tumblers that complement the delicacy of the fabric.

A wide border of double-layer organdy adds a deeper white edging to the cloth. This is further embellished with winding stems of leaves made with ribbon appliqué. The central veins on the leaves are made with simple machine stitching in white. This method of appliqué is quick and very easy to achieve once you have mastered the basic technique. Practice this on a scrap piece of fabric before embarking on the actual cloth. The finished cloth is 52 × 43 in (132 × 109 cm).

1 Make pattern pieces for the four border pieces as follows: for the side border draw a line on paper 52 in (132 cm) long to make the outside edge. Draw another line parallel to and 4¾ in (12 cm) away from the outside edge line to make the inside edge, making a mark 4¾ in (12 cm) in from each end. Join this mark on the inside edge to the end of the outside edge at both ends to shape the mitered corners. Add ¾ in (15 mm) seam allowance on all sides, shaping the ends on the inner and outer edges to follow the slope of the mitre when folded over. Make the end border pattern piece in exactly the same way but with the outside edge line 43 in (109 cm) long.

2 Cut out a rectangle of organdy 53 × 45 in (135 × 112 cm) for the main part of the cloth, plus two side and two end border pieces. With right sides facing, pin and stitch the four border pieces together at the miters, leaving the seam allowance on outside and inside edges free, to make a frame. Trim and press the seams flat. Stay stitch along the inside edge of the border ⅝ in (13 mm) in from the edge. Press the inside edge seam allowance to the wrong side and trim to ¼ in (5 mm).

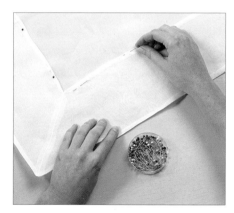

3 With right side of border to wrong side of cloth, pin the border to the main piece, matching outside edges and stitch. Trim seam to ⅝ in (13 mm) and turn to right side. Pin the inside border edge to the main piece and top-stitch close to the fold, then press.

4 On pattern paper draw a gently waving line (copy the template) to fit within the side of the tablecloth, inside the border. Draw leaves evenly spaced within the curves. Draw another wavy line with leaves in the same way to fit within the ends of the tablecloth. Place the pattern underneath the cloth and trace the design lightly on to all sides of the organdy using a washable marker pen.

5 Turn under the end of the ribbon and pin to one end of one of the wavy lines on the cloth. Stitch the ribbon to the cloth following the curves, twisting and slightly pleating the ribbon as you go until all four wavy lines are complete.

6 Stitch the ribbon over the leaf shapes in the same way, twisting it more acutely at the corners to make the points. Machine-stitch a central vein with smaller veins coming off it, using straight rows of stitching in white.

ELDER BLOSSOM FRITTERS AND CORDIAL

THERE IS NO MORE refreshing drink than elder blossom cordial, with its special combination of fresh lemons and the scented blooms of this early summer shrub. The unusual fritters are also infused with the fragrance of elder blossoms and make the perfect accompaniment to elder blossom cordial. They are delicious served hot dredged with superfine sugar. Always pick fresh blossoms that are growing well away from the roadside.

CAUTION: While elderberries are edible, their leaves, bark and roots contain a glucoside that *can* produce hydrocyanic acid. This breaks down in the body and can cause cyanide poisoning.

ELDER BLOSSOM CORDIAL

2 lb 3 oz (1 kg) superfine sugar
1½ pints (850 ml) boiling water
15 large elder blossom heads
1½ oz (45 g) citric acid
2 lemons, sliced

Put the sugar into a heatproof glass bowl and cover with the boiling water. Stir until all the sugar has dissolved. Cut the blossom heads from the green stalks and add the flowers to the sugar solution along with the citric acid and the sliced lemons. Stir together, cover the bowl and leave the mixture to stand for about five days.

Strain the mixture through a sieve into a large jug (line the sieve first with muslin if the mesh is not sufficiently fine). Pour the strained cordial into clean bottles and store in the refrigerator.

To drink, dilute one part cordial with three parts mineral water and serve with slices of lime.

ELDER BLOSSOM FRITTERS

4 oz (115 g) all-purpose flour
1 oz (30 g) superfine sugar
8 fl oz (225 ml) cider
1 oz (30 g) unsalted butter, melted
1 egg white, medium size
Corn oil, for frying
10 elder blossom heads

Sift the flour into a bowl, add the sugar and mix together. Add the cider and the melted butter and beat firmly with a wire whisk, then cover the bowl and let stand for one hour. Whisk the egg white until it is light and fluffy and fold carefully into the batter mixture.

Heat the oil in a deep frying pan. Hold the blossoms by their stalks, dip them into the batter so that they are completely covered and lower them carefully into the hot oil. Fry for two minutes or until golden, turning over once. Drain on paper towels and dredge with sugar before serving. Eat them hot.

HANGING LARDER

Aᴴᴬᴺᴳᴵᴺᴳ ᴸᴬᴿᴰᴱᴿ, suspended in the shade of a tree, helps to keep food cool when eating out of doors.

To make the framework, we used a rectangular wire laundry hanger (the type for drying socks and handkerchiefs) with the pins removed and with two cake cooling trays suspended below on chains. As an alternative, you could use two wire coat hangers to make the top. The roll-up net door keeps flying pests at bay and has ties around the edges for easy opening.

The larder is about 12 in (30 cm) wide, 10 in (25 cm) deep and 22 in (56 cm) high, but you can adapt it to fit any size framework.

To Make the Pattern

The pattern consists of four pieces: the main piece, which forms the sides and the back, the base, the front top and the door flap. To make a pattern for the main piece, measure the height and width of the rectangles that form the sides and back of the larder, then draw the three rectangles on paper adding ¾ in (2 cm) to the side and back edges for the corner edge seams. Extend the front side edges by ¾ in (2 cm) for the seams, then a further 3¾ in (9 cm) for the front side flaps. Measure the depth of the triangles, which will form the top and the sloping sides, then draw the triangles with the top points cut off, on the top of each side and back piece. Add a ½ in (1 cm) seam allowance to the edges of the triangles and along the bottom edge of the main piece.

For the larder base, draw a rectangle to match the width of the sides and the back on the main piece, extending the front edge by 2 in (5 cm) for the front bottom flap. Add a ½ in (1 cm) seam and turning allowance on all four sides.

For the larder front top, draw a triangle to match the back top triangle and extend the base by 2 in (5 cm) for the front top flap. Add a ½ in (1 cm) seam and turning allowance to all sides. For the door flap, draw a rectangle the same size as the larder back but do not add any seam allowance.

YOU WILL NEED

A wire laundry hanger with
the clothespins removed

Two wire cake cooling racks
the same size as the hanger

Pattern paper

Tape measure

4 ft 3 in (1.3 m) length of thin chain

Small round-nosed pliers

10 in (25 cm) length of garden wire

Wire cutters

1 yd (1 m) net fabric,
54 in (140 cm) wide

4 yds (4 m) bias binding,
1 in (2.5 cm) wide

Sewing thread and needle

Scissors and pins

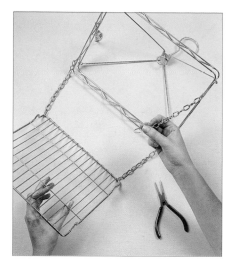

1 Cut the chain into eight 6¼ in (16 cm)
lengths. Cut eight pieces of garden wire
each 1¼ in (3 cm) long. Using round-nosed
pliers, bend each piece of garden wire into S
shapes and attach one to each end of chain,
closing the loops to secure the wire. Attach a
length of chain to each corner of bottom edge
of the laundry hanger in the same way, then
attach the other end of each chain to the
corners of a wire cooling tray and secure to
make the top shelf. Fix another cooling tray
with a chain at each corner in the same way
below the first tray to make the lower shelf.

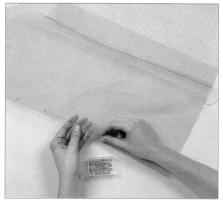

2 Cut out one of each of the pattern pieces
in net. On the main piece, with right
sides facing, fold along the front corner edge
and stitch ½ in (1 cm) from the fold to make
a tuck. Make tucks at the back corner and
other front corner edges in the same way.
Turn under ½ in (1 cm) to the wrong side
along both front side flap edges and stitch.

3 With right sides facing, bring the sides
of a side and back top triangle together
and stitch, leaving a ½ in (1 cm) seam
allowance. Sew the other side top triangle in
the same way. Turn under ½ in (1 cm) to the
wrong side along the front top flap edge and
stitch. With right sides facing, pin and stitch
the front top piece in place in the same way
as before, stitching along both sides of the
triangle.

4 Turn under ½ in (1 cm) to the wrong
side along the front bottom flap and
stitch. With right sides facing, pin the base
to the side and back bottom edges of the main
piece and stitch. Fold the front bottom flap
up to meet the front side flaps and stitch in
place along the base and side edges so the
side flaps are to the front. Fold the front top
flap down to meet the side flaps and stitch in
place along the side folds so the side flaps
are to the front.

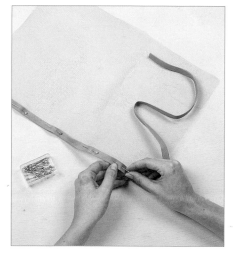

5 Bind all four sides of the door flap with
bias binding, doubled over the door
edges, and stitch in place. Pin and stitch the
door flap in place along the top from edge.
Fold the binding in half lengthways and
stitch close to the edge to make ties for the
door. Cut the binding into ten 10 in (25 cm)
lengths and sew them in corresponding pairs
two down each side and one at the center
front of the base. Bind the edges of the hole
formed where the top triangles meet with bias
binding. Place the hanging shelf arrangement
inside the net cover to complete.

OUTDOOR LIGHTING

THESE BEAUTIFUL paper bag lanterns with their pretty cut-out images of moths give an ethereal glow on a still summer's evening. The motif is apt, as subtly decorated moths arrive at night to pollinate the pale and most scented flowers. Place these lanterns on outdoor steps, along a garden patio or around the lawn to create a truly magical effect for an outdoor party.

MOTH-CUTOUT LANTERNS

THESE MAGICAL LANTERNS with their clever light and dark moth motifs take only minutes to make using simple tools and equipment. You will need to obtain fairly strong brown paper bags as these stand up without support. The light is produced by placing votive candles in glass jars inside the paper bag – two or even three candles in each bag produce a brighter glow.

YOU WILL NEED

Large, strong paper bags

Template (see page 186)

Pencil

Cutting mat

Craft knife

Paper glue

Glass jars

Votive candles

1 Place the template over the top half of the bag and carefully draw around it with a sharp pencil, taking particular care around the antennae.

2 Remove the template and slide the cutting mat inside the bag (to ensure you only cut through one layer of paper). Use the craft knife to cut around the pencil lines of the moth shape.

3 Lift out the moth shape and then stick it in place on the lower half of the bag using the paper glue. Take care to position it centrally beneath the upper cutout moth.

4 Remove the cutting mat and open up the bag. Put the candles into small glass jars and insert them into the base of the bag, ready for lighting when dusk falls.

Lights for a Balmy Evening

RIGHT: *A wonderful sense of peace and serenity can be created with floating candles. Here a marble bowl carved in the shape of a lotus flower has been filled with white candles surrounded by tiny white roses in a pool of water. Use it as a centerpiece on a supper table decorated with a white theme.*

LEFT: *These glimmering outdoor lights are made from small glass jars containing votives with handles created from copper wire threaded with coppery pink glass beads. The decorative leaves attached to the front of the jars are simply cut from copper foil, which has been decorated with leaf veins using a sewer's tracing wheel.*

ABOVE: *Often the simplest ideas are the most effective, and this crowded group of fragrant beeswax candles loosely arranged on the patinated top of an old metal table against a stone wall creates a vibrant source of light as evening darkens into night.*

ABOVE: *These exotic metal candlelit lanterns are made in Morocco or India from tin, brass or recycled, highly decorated oil cans and are usually inexpensive to buy. Here a number have been lit and suspended in a small tree over a garden seat, making a perfect setting for a quiet conversation or evening meditation.*

The Garden Room

DURING THE LONG SUMMER months, the house extends into the garden and the garden lends its flowery presence to the house. Life changes for a welcome while, and meals are taken outside until late into the evening when the heady scent of summer blossoms grows stronger to attract the pollinating moths. There's no need to visit the flower shop now, as baskets of blooms can be gathered to grace each room and yet more can be taken as beautiful offerings for cherished friends. The curious thing is you do not even need to have a large garden for this altered life. Just a few well-planted pots around the patio door will suffice.

Plant Containers

ABOVE: *A good way to display plants in pots is to stack them on a tiered plant stand or étagère so they all have access to the sun. Here a collection of ridged and fluted galvanized pots has been planted with herbs. Try not to make your arrangement look too formal and perhaps introduce one or two different containers, such as the glazed pot or the rusty urn seen here.*

RIGHT: *African marigolds tempt with their dazzling array of oranges and yellows, but finding a way of avoiding the usual municipal or suburban planting method can be a challenge. They look best massed together against a bright background, a painted shed wall for example. Here they have been planted into a maroon enamel bucket but would look equally striking in a colorful plastic bucket. Don't forget to add drainage holes to the base.*

LEFT: *Create a Mediterranean feel by planting vibrantly colored geraniums, osteospermums and verbenas in empty olive oil or olive cans. These are discarded by delicatessens and restaurants and are often stunning in color and design. Simply make some drainage holes in the base with a bradawl or hammer and nail, add a little gravel, fill with compost and they are ready to plant. They look stunning against a brightly painted wall.*

ABOVE: *Little mounds of alpine plants look charming when planted into pretty old teacups. Use them to form part of an unusual summer table setting — they can remain in the cups as long as they don't become waterlogged. This can be a risk as there are no holes in the base of a teacup so just water occasionally with a few drops.*

SCALLOPED WINDOW BOX

SIMPLE WOODEN PLANTERS and window boxes can be decorated by adding a scalloped edging cut from lead strip (or other metal). Lead, though toxic, has traditionally been used to make garden containers as it is extremely durable and weathers beautifully. Lead strip is available from building supply stores and is easy to cut with tin snips. Paint the wooden container with a colored wood stain before adding the edging, as this will also help to protect the wood from the elements, and drill some holes in the base to provide good drainage. Wear gloves when working with lead.

YOU WILL NEED

A wooden window box or planter

Ruler, pencil and paper

Wine glass or tumbler

Scissors

Lead strip 6 in (15 cm) wide

Bradawl and hammer

Tin snips

¾ × ⅛ in (20 × 3 mm) galvanized clout nails

Gloves

Cream-colored paint and a soft cloth (optional)

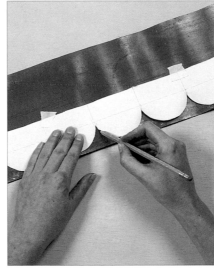

1 Measure around the top edge of the container. Make a paper template for the scalloped edging to fit around the container top and 1½ in (4 cm) deep. Divide the template into equal parts for the scallops, and draw around the bottom of a glass to make even curves 1¼ in (3 cm) deep. Cut out the template and place it on the lead strip. Draw around the template to make a continuous strip to fit all along the top edge of the planter.

2 Make a hole with a bradawl at each point where the scallops meet (the lead is very soft and will puncture easily). Wearing gloves when handling the lead, cut out the scalloped edging using tin snips and working from the bottom of each curve up toward the bradawl hole in each direction.

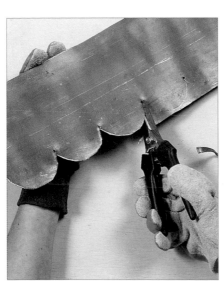

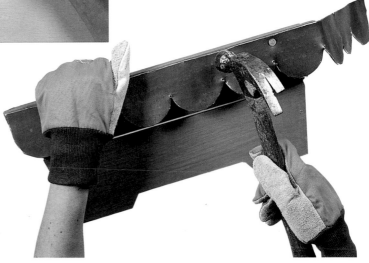

3 Place the edging along the top of the planter and fix in position with evenly spaced nails. To age the lead instantly, rub cream-colored paint into the metal with a soft cloth, wiping off any excess. Leave to dry thoroughly before planting in the container.

WIREWORK PLANT SUPPORTS

THESE ORNATE TWISTED WIRE plant supports are surprisingly easy to create and make a striking frame for special conservatory plants. There was a thriving wire industry in France and England in the nineteenth century in response to the demand for decorative pieces for domestic use. Elaborate conservatories filled with wire furniture, plant stands and hanging baskets were popular and, outside in the garden, larger constructions were made in the form of trellises, fencing and rose arches. Although the industry has declined, there is now a revival of interest in decorative wirework and this project provides a splendid introduction to the subject.

YOU WILL NEED
3 rolls of galvanized wire, ¹⁄₁₆ in (1.60 mm), .05 in (1.25 mm) and .03 in (0.75 mm) thick
Wire cutters
Hand drill
Bent-nosed pliers
Piece of dowel, approximately 12 in (30 cm) long and ¾ in (2 cm) in diameter

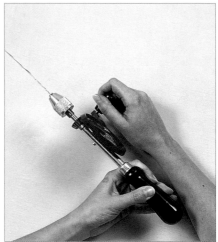

1 In order to achieve the correct lengths of twisted wire, you need to cut the wire double the desired length plus a little extra (up to 25 percent) to allow for the twisting. Cut a 5 yd (4.5 m) length of the ¹⁄₁₆ in (1.60 mm) wire and three 4¼ yd (4 m) lengths of the .05 in (1.25 mm) wire. Bend the wire in the middle around a fixed point such as a sturdy door handle or banister. Feed the two cut ends into the chuck of the drill, tighten and wind the drill handle until the required twist has been achieved. Repeat with all lengths. Release from the drill and cut the wire away from the fixed point. There is usually some extra twist released at this point so take care that the wire does not spring back.

2 Cut the ¹⁄₁₆ in (1.60 mm) twisted wire in half. Using the bent-nosed pliers, begin to twist the spiral decoration at one end. Stretch the wire against your thumb and evenly work the wire into a spiral shape with an 3¼ in (8 cm) diameter. Repeat this technique on the other length of wire, matching the size of the spiral. Bend the straight wire away from the spiral at 45 degrees and curve gently into a straight section in line with the center of the spiral.

3 Take a short length of the .03 in (0.75 mm) wire and bind the two spirals tightly together three times. To finish twist the two ends, and cut away the excess with the wire cutters.

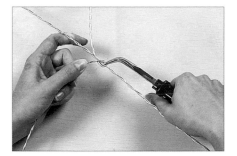

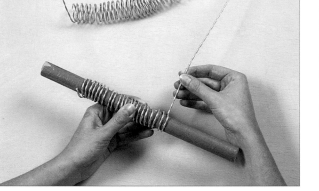

5 To make the coils, wind each remaining 2 yd (2 m) length of the .05 in (1.25 mm) twisted wire around the dowel. You will need a length containing 18 coils, but wind a few extra around to ease manipulation.

4 Using the twisted .05 in (1.25 mm) wire, now measuring 2 yds (2 m), place the middle 8 in (20 cm) section across the two spiral-ended pieces. Twist tightly once around the uprights and cross each remaining length, fixing in the same way every 6 in (15 cm) down the upright frame, twisting the ends tightly four times around the uprights. Cut off the excess. This makes four fixings on each side, including top and base.

6 Slide the coils off the dowel and flatten them by pulling each one out with one hand and pressing it flat with the other. Make the two lengths as even as possible.

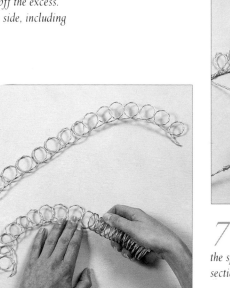

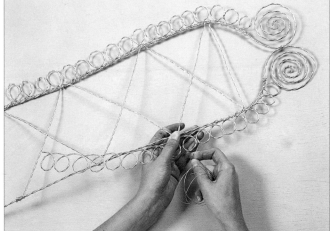

7 Bind the flattened coils along each upright side using the .03 in (0.75 mm) untwisted wire. Stretch the 18 loops so they reach just below the spirals at the top and just above the last attachment of the criss-crossed section. Cut off any extra and wind the binding wire tightly to finish.

PAINTED BIRD HOUSE

THIS CHARMING lead-roofed bird house will decorate your garden as well as provide a secure nesting box for small birds. It needs to be set upon a tall garden post well away from cats. The nesting box stands on a flat base that can double as a feeding table in winter. The decorative roof and table trim has been cut from a length of lead flashing. Lead is toxic so you need to wear gloves when handling it. It is, however, very easy to cut and work with as it is one of the softest and most pliable of metals.

YOU WILL NEED

Cut sections of timber ¾ in (1.5 cm) thick: two side sections 6 × 4⅓ in (15 × 11 cm) and two end sections 4⅓ × 4⅓ in (11 × 11 cm) with a 6⅔ in (17 cm) gable (see templates on page 189)

Base 10¼ × 8¼ in (26 × 21 cm), cut from MDF (medium density fiberboard) ¾ in (2 cm) thick

Internal base 6 × 3¼ in (15 × 8 cm), cut from MDF ½ in (1 cm) thick

Eggcup or similar round object with a diameter of 1¼ in (3 cm)

Pencil

Drill with a large bit

Sandpaper

Woodworking glue

Hammer and panel pins 1¼ in (3 cm) long

Blue external timber paint and paintbrush

Protective gloves

Short roll of standard lead flashing

Galvanized flat-headed nails

Very strong scissors and pinking shears

Bradawl

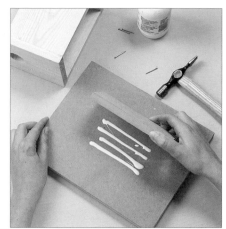

1 Cut the two side and two end sections from the timber (a good timber supplier may do this for you), and draw around the eggcup to mark the place for the entrance hole as shown. Use a large drill bit to drill the hole and sand the edges to finish.

2 Put a line of glue along the ends of the side sections and position the gable ends. Nail in place using two nails on each side.

3 Put four lines of glue onto the center of the larger MDF base and stick the smaller piece of MDF centrally over it. Allow the glue to dry

4 When the glue has dried, fit the assembled sides over this internal base section and nail to secure, using two nails on each side.

5 Cover the outside of the house and base with two coats of the timber paint. Also paint the top edges of the assembled house and underneath the base table.

6 Wearing gloves, cut two pieces of lead 5½ × 7¼ in (14 × 18.5 cm). Draw a scalloped edge along one long side using the same template as for the hole, and cut around these shapes using the strong scissors. Cut out a roof ridge section using the pinking shears to make a decorative edge measuring 7 × 2 in (18 × 5 cm), and bend it lengthways along the middle.

7 Nail the two sections of the roof in place with the galvanized nails. To do this, first make a guide hole through the lead into the timber with the bradawl. Put the two lower nails on each side in first, add the roof ridge and finish by nailing the remaining nails through the two thicknesses to secure the roof. Cut a strip of lead 2 in (5 cm) wide and long enough to reach around the table base. Create a scalloped edge as before and fix around the base of the table in the same way using the galvanized nails.

Summer Blooms

LEFT: *When arranging flowers it is important to consider the shape of your container, as this will affect the final outcome of the display. The long narrow opening of this trophy vase is ideal for the pleasantly unruly stems of this wonderful dark clematis. Letting one or two stems with buds tumble over the rim of the vase makes for a charmingly natural arrangement.*

RIGHT: *Almost the most evocative flowers of summer, these old-fashioned roses in their range of soft pinks produce the ultimate flower arrangement. It is best to display them naturally with the addition of just a few garden flowers to help give shape to the arrangement. Here alchemilla, stachys and polemonium have been used sparingly. A simple ribbed china jug completes the picture.*

ABOVE: *These tightly bound little bunches of sweetly smelling summer flowers are known as tuzzy-muzzies. Gather together a selection of fragrant herbs and flowers and tie loosely with a pretty ribbon. They can be dried by hanging them upside down in an airy place, thus preserving them for ever. Tuzzy-muzzies became popular as fashionable accessories in the mid-nineteenth century and were carried by genteel ladies. They were often presented to an admirer, with each flower having a symbolic significance.*

ABOVE: *These charming little arrangements are created quickly and are just the thing to adorn a table or windowsill in a newly prepared guest room. Using highly scented flowers such as honeysuckle and jasmine means a small arrangement creates a powerful effect. The subtle pinks in the flowers match the pink luster glaze on the antique mugs beautifully.*

ABOVE: *Who can resist the fresh fragrance of sweet peas? With their pretty shaped petals of pastel colors and unforgettable scent, they should only be displayed on their own. It is therefore important to choose the perfect container. This globular-shaped green ceramic vase is ideal as the narrow opening holds the delicate stems firmly in place while the broader body of the shape allows for an evenly balanced arrangement of flowers.*

RIGHT: *Some flowers are so striking they are best displayed alone in a very simple container. Here the metallic gray of the galvanized pot complements the clear blue of the frilly petals of these scabious.*

COPPER HERB LABELS

PLANT LABELS or identification tags have traditionally been used in rather grand gardens. They are usually made from zinc or copper as both metals are noncorrosive and copper, in particular, takes on a subtle green patina called verdigris when exposed to the elements. The copper foil used in this project is thin enough to cut with scissors and the name of the plant has been written onto the soft surface of the metal with a dried-up ballpoint pen.

YOU WILL NEED

Roll of thin copper foil

Template (see page 188)

Transparent tape

Ballpoint pen

Sewing tracing wheel

Small pointed scissors

1 Place the card template on the foil and stick in place with transparent tape. Place on a wad of tissue paper — this will protect your work surface. Draw around the template with the ballpoint pen, pressing firmly to transfer the design.

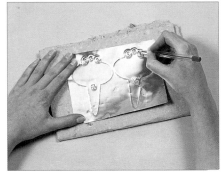

2 Remove the template and, still using the pen, draw a star in the middle section at the top and at the top of the stem. Draw two tight spirals on each side of the top star.

3 Use the tracing wheel to make the embossed dotted line by rolling the wheel firmly around the oval shape and then down either side of the stem. Roll a central line up the stem, stopping at the star.

4 Turn the label over so the pattern you have drawn on the other side appears as a raised design. Using the ballpoint pen write the name of the plant (here we have used the Latin names for herbs).

5 Finally, cut around the shape with the pointed scissors leaving a 1/16 in (1 mm) margin from the ballpoint line.

GLASS FLOWER TANK

THIS INGENIOUS WAY OF customizing a glass flower tank provides a lovely way to display a number of special flowers without all the stems falling to one side of the vase. Holes have been made with an eyelet tool in easy-to-use, thick aluminum foil, which is available by mail order from specialist craft suppliers. If you wish, make smaller holes with a different sized eyelet kit or adapt the idea for use over any glass container — try it on prettily shaped jam jars, turning the metal over the sides in a scalloped design.

YOU WILL NEED

Sturdy square or rectangular
glass vase

———

Thick aluminum foil

———

Ballpoint pen

———

Pot lid to use as template for
drawing curves

———

Scissors

———

Ruler

———

Eyelet hole maker from a large
eyelet kit

———

Wooden board

———

Hammer

———

Hole punch

1 Lay the vase upside down on a piece of the metal foil that has been cut to leave at least a 2 in (5 cm) border all around the vase rim. Draw around the rim with the ballpoint pen, making an indented line to mark the shape.

2 Remove the vase and, using the pot lid as a template, draw equal curves out from each straight side toward the edge of the foil. Remember to press firmly so the indented line is clear. Carefully cut around the marked curves with the scissors.

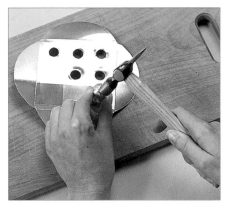

3 Using the pen and ruler, mark the central section into nine equal squares. Place the base part of the eyelet cutter on a wooden board and lie the metal on top, positioning the eyelet centrally under one of the nine sections. Place the top part of the cutter exactly above the lower part and bang very firmly with the hammer two or three times to cut the hole.

4 Repeat until you have made nine holes. Now make a row of small holes around each curved edge with the hole punch.

5 Bend the curved sides up at right angles against the edge of the ruler and fit in place on top of the glass vase.

AUTUMN

Halloween

T HE END OF OCTOBER is an exciting time for children with the traditions of "trick or treat" and spooky lanterns carved from the fiery colored shapes of pumpkins harvested from newly frosted fields and gardens.

As with many ancient celebrations, Halloween has complicated origins. It coincides with the pagan festival marking of the end of summer and its fruitfulness. In early Christian times, October 31 was designated as the Eve of All Hallows, the time when the souls of the dead were remembered. Rutabagas or turnips were scooped out, filled with a candle and lit in windows, acting as glowing guides for souls to find their former homes.

Today witches and ghosts predominate, with children carrying bags and traveling from house to house to collect treats or else play tricks. A friendly house is symbolized by the jack-o'-lantern glowing in the window.

LITTLE GEM TABLE LIGHTS

THESE UNUSUAL little candleholders are quite simple to make and will last for a number of days if kept airtight in a fridge between lighting. The use of a lino-cutting tool is the key to the bold design and the dark green peel is cut away in spirals stars or stripes to reveal the yellow flesh beneath. This allows the warm light of the candle to glow through. As they are so small and quick to make, each Halloween guest can have his or her very own.

YOU WILL NEED

White grease pencil

Selection of small
gem squashes

Votive candles

Craft knife or small kitchen knife

Teaspoon

V-shaped lino-cutting tool

1 Using the grease pencil, mark a circle around the top of the squash using a candle as a template. Cut along this line with a craft knife or kitchen knife. Remove and discard the "lid."

2 Scoop out the flesh and seeds inside the squash with the spoon so that the walls are no more than ¼ in (5 mm) thick.

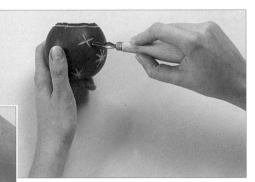

3 Use the lino-cutting tool to cut a line around the rim of the opening. Hold the tool firmly and always cut in a direction away from yourself.

4 Make the eight-pointed star shapes by cutting four lines, each ¾ in (2 cm) long, the first two crossing each other at right angles, the second two crossing them at an angle of 45 degrees. Pop a candle into the base of each squash ready for lighting.

GOURD LANTERNS

OUTDOOR LANTERNS really do create an enchanting atmosphere for outdoor Halloween parties or to decorate a tree close to the house. Bell cups are small dried gourds that are sold for use in dried flower arrangements, usually attached to sticks that are easily removed. They can be found in either a pale natural wood color or sometimes dyed in bright or deep colors. As well as being useful for floral displays, they make colorful covers for fairy lights. Painting the insides of the cups in bright metallic colors will add an iridescent shimmer when the lights are turned on.

YOU WILL NEED

Dried gourds
(one for each light on the string)

Metallic paints

Brushes

Scrap piece of cardboard

Bradawl

Plastic paper

Scissors

A string of outdoor fairy lights

Epoxy resin

1 Make sure that the insides of the gourds are clean and dust-free. Paint the insides of each gourd with metallic paint, alternating the colors and leave to dry.

2 Place the gourd on a piece of card to protect the work surface and make a hole in the base of each gourd with a bradawl. Start by piercing the woody base from the right side and enlarge the hole bit by bit. The hole needs to be just big enough for the light bulb to go through.

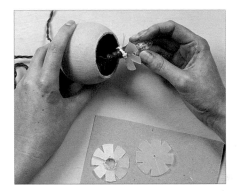

3 Cut a pair of 1¾ in (4.5 cm) circles out of plastic paper for every light. Make a hole in the center of one plastic circle just big enough for the wire flex to go through. Make a larger hole in the second circle, big enough to fit around the base of a light. Cut through each circle from the outside edge to the central hole and snip out small V shapes around the outside. Pull a lightbulb through the hole in the gourd base and place the circle with the larger hole around the base of the light. Apply glue to the underside of the circle and stick in place inside the gourd, pulling the light and flex back into the cup.

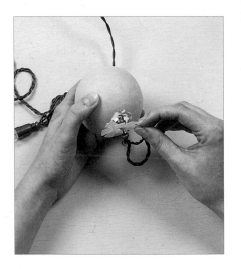

4 Place the second circle with the smaller hole around the flex at the outer base of the gourd and glue in place to secure the light inside. Fix the other lights in place inside the gourds in the same way.

PAPER CUTOUT CATS

P APER CUTOUT CATS make an unusual evening window display at Halloween. Simple and undecorated, they are cut from a length of white paper that has been folded zigzag fashion. This popular technique is particularly suitable for children to experiment with and it lends itself to all sorts of themed images. Witches on broomsticks, pumpkins with leery grins and, when you become more adept at cutting out complicated images, perhaps a menacing spider in a web could all be produced. The paper used is white cartridge as it needs to be thick enough to support itself when cut but thin enough for you to be able to cut through a number of layers at a time.

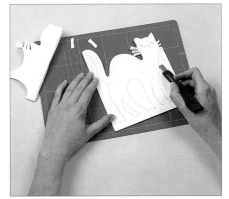

1 Cut the paper into a rectangle 8 in (20 cm) wide by 30 in (75 cm) long. Fold neatly into five sections concertina-style, each section measuring 6 in (15 cm) wide.

2 Place the template on the top fold and hold in place with paper clips. The base, tail and whiskers should be against the folds on either side. Draw around neatly with the pencil to transfer the outline on to the paper.

3 Lay the folded paper on the cutting mat and cut around the pencil lines. If the knife blade doesn't cut easily through the five layers of paper, cut two or three at a time.

4 After all the cut-away sections have been removed, open up the folds to reveal the five cats. You can make a longer row by using longer paper or sticking two rows together.

BOUNCING SKELETON DOLL

THESE SPOOKY polymer clay skeleton dolls are very easy to make and they will last forever. Bring them out each year and hang them from door handles or suspend them on ribbons in lighted windows. When moved, the coiled wire arms and legs bounce in an entertaining way. They are inspired by the inventive and humorous skeleton figures produced in Mexico around the time of the famous Day of the Dead festival, which coincides with Halloween.

YOU WILL NEED

Roll of galvanized wire,
.03 in (0.75 mm) thick

Long knitting needle

Wire cutters

Polymer clay –
two 2½ oz (65 g) packs of white,
one 2½ oz (65 g) pack of black

Modeling tool

Baking tray

Length of ribbon

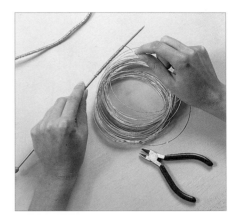

1 To make the springs for the arms and legs, wind the wire tightly directly from the roll onto the top third of the knitting needle. Push the wire down the needle as the coil increases in length. You will probably have to wind two whole lengths of the needle to make the required amount for the doll.

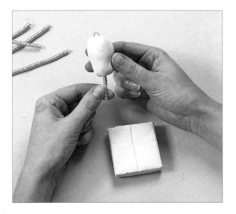

2 When the coils are finished, cut two lengths of 5 in (13 cm) for the legs, two lengths of 4½ in (11 cm) for the arms and one 1½ in (4 cm) for the neck. Take approximately half of one block of the white polymer clay, soften in your hands and mold into a skull shape. Push a small loop of wire into the top of the skull to act as a hook and twist the neck length into the base.

3 Using smaller pieces of white clay, mold oval-shaped pieces around the end of the arm and leg wire coils to make the hands and feet.

4 Use all the second block of the white clay to make the body shape. Now roll small pieces of the black clay between your fingers and push the strips into the white to make the bones of the skeleton. Add the facial features as well.

5 Push the arms and the legs into place, using the modeling tool to make the initial holes and to firm the clay around the wire coil so that it stays securely in place. When all is completed, carefully lay the doll on a baking tray and bake in a warm oven according to the temperature specified on the clay packet for 20–30 minutes. Allow the doll to cool, remove from the baking tray and thread a ribbon through the loop at the top of the skull.

HALLOWEEN MASK

HALLOWEEN IS AN EERIE FESTIVAL popular among children, who, generally love to dress up in spooky clothes and wear frightening masks. This leafy mask has a pagan feel, reminiscent of the cult of the Green man, an ancient god of the natural world. This kind of half-mask is easily obtainable and was much favored in earlier times for masked balls as it easy to wear, covering only half the face while still managing to fully disguise the wearer.

1 Remove the softened leaves from the spray and grade them according to size. Apply a small amount of glue to the mask and begin by sticking the larger leaves symmetrically along the top of the mask. Make sure each leaf overlaps the edge of the mask by one-third. Add the next row of slightly smaller leaves, overlapping the first.

2 Continue sticking the leaves over the mask in this way, starting with the larger leaves and overlapping decreasingly smaller ones until the whole mask is covered. Add very small ones horizontally along the top edge of the eye holes. Use smaller leaves on the molded nose section. The last leaf to be applied will be in the center of the nose.

YOU WILL NEED

Spray of glycerin-dipped
oak or beech leaves

Molded half-mask

Clear adhesive, or glue gun
if available

Small scissors

3 Use the small scissors to cut neatly along the bottom edge of the eye. This delineates the wearer's eye as well as making it easier to see through.

CANDIED APPLES

B Y THE END OF AUTUMN most of the apple crop has been gathered. The apples that will store well have been cleaned, wrapped and left in a cool, dry place to last into the winter months, while the remaining fruit can be eaten fresh or can be used in a vast range of sweet and savory recipes. Traditionally cooked with spices, apples are versatile enough to serve as an appetizing dessert or as a sauce to accompany a meat dish. There are so many ways of preparing and eating apples at this time of year, but these delicious candied apples are a traditional children's favorite.

Choose unblemished eating apples. The quantities given here will make eight candied apples, which will keep for a couple of days if wrapped in parchment paper and stored in a dry place. Children should not make this recipe without an adult present, as melted sugar can be dangerously hot.

Wash the apples well, remove the stalks and dry thoroughly. Push a wooden skewer or popsicle stick through the core into the center of each apple. Measure 1 lb (450 g) sugar, 3 heaping tbsp (50 ml) treacle and ¼ pint (150 ml) water into a saucepan and stir over low heat until the sugar has dissolved, then increase the heat and bring quickly to a boil. Cook rapidly at this heat until the mixture begins to caramelize or until a temperature of 310°F (154°C) is reached on a sugar thermometer. Remove the pan from the heat, carefully tilt it sideways and dip in each apple, turning it until it is completely covered with the caramel. Remove from the pan, drain and let set on a sheet of parchment paper. Repeat with the other apples.

Harvest Supper

WITH THE SUMMER ENDING and the nights beginning to draw in, this must surely be the most bountiful time of year for the fruits of the fields and orchards. A harvest dinner traditionally celebrates the changing of the seasons, the gathering in of the harvest and the richness of this time. Food needs to be hearty and warming and the colors should reflect the hues that surround us as the leaves on the trees turn to all the shades of amber and softly fall to the ground.

AUTUMN FRUITS

ONCE THE WARM DAYS of summer are over, the first frosts threaten. Our thoughts turn to bringing the autumn harvest in. The rosy apples, the generously shaped pears and the last of the season's blackberries need to be gathered and stored for the winter.

Try to pick the nuts before the marauding squirrels have them for their winter store. Rosehips for jam and syrup should be collected after the first light frost has softened their vermilion flesh. To make sure the fruit stores well throughout. the winter, remember to collect and pick on a dry day.

Use only unblemished fruit for storing. Windfall apples or bruised pears can still be used for baking in delicious spiced puddings. You only need to spend a few days gathering ripened fruit, making jams, pickles and chutneys and bottling fruit to have an appetizing supply to last you right through the winter.

HEDGEROW HARVEST

THE CLEAR BRIGHT BLUES, yellows, purples and pinks of the hedgerow flowers in summer are now gone, their place taken by the woolly seeds of the wild clematis, sprays of sparkling red rosehips and a few sprays of tightly clenched, unripe blackberries. Hedgerow trees really come into their own at this time of year, in particular with the fiery color of the spindle berries and the tinted leaves of the wild viburnum.

Take a leisurely walk down a country lane and you will still find plenty to gather into stunning, deliberately unrestrained bunches to decorate the home.

SEED PACKETS

IF YOU ARE A PERSON who gathers seed from your own or a friend's garden at the end of the summer, then this project is perfect for you. These envelopes are simple to construct and make ideal gifts.

Commercially grown seeds can be extremely expensive to buy and packets often contain very few seeds. A few basic rules need to be followed when storing seeds: pick them on a dry day, hang them up to dry in a warm place if they are still in their seed pods, and pack and store in dry conditions. The enemies of seeds are damp and mold – in fact commercially packed seeds will have been treated with a fungicide so if you collect and store seeds in the best conditions, you can manage without the help of chemicals.

YOU WILL NEED

Sheet of handmade plant paper

Template (see page 190)

Sharp pencil

Small scissors

Paper glue

Scrap of recycled green paper

Small glassine envelopes

Crayon

1 Cut a rectangle from the plant paper measuring approximately 10 × 6 in (25 × 15 cm). Lay the template over it and draw around with the pencil.

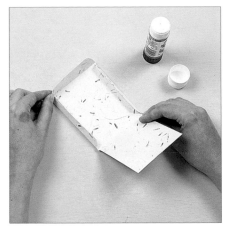

2 Fold up the three sides to make the tabs as shown by the dotted lines on the template. Apply glue to the two vertical sides. Fold the envelope in half along the line indicated on the template and press to secure.

3 Draw a leaf shape slightly smaller than the envelope front on to the green paper and cut out with the scissors. Stick in place on the front of the envelope.

4 Carefully pack the seeds into the glassine envelopes, seal and slide into the larger envelope, seal again and store in a dry place. Write the plant name in crayon on the front of the envelope.

The Harvest Table

RIGHT: *Autumn leaves in wonderful shades of russet and amber make useful place markers. Guests' names are written on leaves in gold or silver felt-tip pen and displayed at every place setting.*

LEFT: *A gourd makes an unusual container for autumn blooms. Choose a colorful gourd with a flat base that will sit steady on the table, or cut the base flat and place the gourd on a saucer. Make a hole in the center large enough to hold a jam jar and arrange seasonal flowers in it, such as orange lanterns (physalis), Michaelmas daisies and rosehips.*

ABOVE: *Make the most of the produce of the season by including it as part of the table decoration. Beautiful russet leaves from a sumac tree radiate like the rays of the sun from the center of a wooden platter with a wild crab apple placed between each leaf around the rim. It makes a spectacular focal point for a simple wooden bowl of chutney.*

BELOW: *Pumpkin risotto makes a more colorful alternative to mushroom risotto but is made in the same way. Serve small portions as a first course for six people or as a hearty main dish for four people.*

A small pumpkin or butternut squash
Salt and pepper
2 tbsp olive oil
2 oz (60 g) butter
3 shallots, chopped
10 oz (280 g) Carnaroli rice
1 glass of white wine, warmed
Up to 1¾ pints (1 liter) vegetable stock
2 oz (60 g) freshly grated Parmesan cheese

Preheat the oven to 450°F (230°C). Slice and cut the flesh away from the skin of the pumpkin and remove the seeds. Cut the flesh into 1 in (2.5 cm) chunks, place in a roasting pan, season well, then drizzle with olive oil, turning over the pumpkin to coat the chunks. Roast in the oven for 30–40 minutes until the pumpkin is tender and still holding its shape, turning it gently halfway through cooking. Remove from the oven and set aside. Heat half the butter in a pan, add the shallots and sauté until soft. Stir in the rice to coat with butter and a third of the pumpkin, then pour the wine over the rice. Stir until the liquid is absorbed, then add the stock a ladleful at a time, waiting for it to be absorbed between additions and stirring frequently. When the rice is al dente and creamy, remove from the heat and gently stir in the remaining butter, pumpkin and cheese. Cover the pan for 2 minutes, then gently stir again and serve.

ABOVE: *Sloe gin is a delicious liqueur. A sumptuous deep maroon color, it is ready to drink in just a few weeks but benefits from being left longer for the flavor to mature. Small bottles of sloe gin make lovely home-made gifts.*

Prick 5 lb (2.2 kg) sloes with a sharp fork and place them in a large wide-necked bottle or plastic jar. Add 1 lb (450 g) sugar and one bottle of gin and cover tightly. Leave in a dark cupboard for at least 8 weeks, shaking occasionally to dissolve the sugar. Strain the gin off the fruits and pour it into clean bottles.

BRAIDED LOAF

No ONE CAN RESIST the smell of freshly baked bread wafting through the kitchen, and any extra effort involved in home baking is always worthwhile. It also provides an opportunity to add unusual grains, seed and dried fruits to the dough to make loaves that cannot be matched by store-bought varieties.

Kneading the dough is a very tactile and soothing pastime and it can be molded into lots of different decorative shapes. As well as a wholesome braid, you can bake homestyle breads in terra-cotta pots, scrubbed, oiled and dusted with flour prior to use. Or roll a quarter of the dough into a small ball, roll the remainder into a larger, slightly flattened round, then lightly press the small ball on the top for a traditional cottage loaf. Brush all over with beaten egg or milk for a glazed finish.

YOU WILL NEED
Approximately 12 fl oz (360 ml) hot tap water
1 tbsp honey
2 level tsp dried yeast
2 tsp salt
1 lb (450 g) whole wheat flour
4 tsp sunflower oil
4 oz (100 g) sunflower seeds
Beaten egg

1 Measure 3 fl oz (75 ml) water into a measuring jug and stir in the honey. Sprinkle the dried yeast into the liquid and stir, then leave covered in a warm place for 15 minutes until a froth has formed. In a bowl, mix the salt into the flour and add the oil, rubbing it through the dry mixture with your fingertips. Add the sunflower seeds, keeping a few aside to decorate the top. Make a well in the center and pour in the yeast liquid and the rest of the water, adjusting the amount as necessary.

Mix with your hands until the dough leaves the sides of the bowl, then transfer to a floured surface and knead until the dough becomes elastic with a smooth surface. Mold the dough into a round and place in an oiled bowl, cover with a kitchen towel and leave in a warm place until it has risen and doubled in size.

2 Knock the dough back down and place on a floured surface. Divide it into three equal portions and roll each one on a floured surface to make long sausage shapes.

3 Working from the middle of the braid out toward the ends, twist the three lengths together to form a plump, evenly braided loaf, tucking in the dough at the ends to secure.

4 Place the loaf on an oiled baking sheet, brush the top with beaten egg to glaze and sprinkle with the remaining sunflower seeds. Leave in a warm place until it has risen. Preheat the oven to 450°F (230°C) and bake in the middle of the oven for 35–45 minutes until it sounds hollow when tapped underneath and the surface is golden. Cool on a wire rack.

Preserving and Storing

EACH SEASON brings its own individual pleasures and in autumn we harvest, gather, store and preserve fruit and produce from field, wood and garden. Wild fungi are gathered, cleaned, carefully identified and dried. Nuts are picked from the laden trees. Jams and chutneys are made from ripened fruit and the last green vegetables, and herb-flavored oils are bottled all in preparation for the winter. Although now we all have access to fresh produce all year round, we still derive enormous satisfaction from these traditional seasonal activities.

Storing Autumn Produce

LEFT: *Apples and pears that are suitable for storing through the winter need to be unblemished and picked on a dry day. They should be stored in a cool dry room and each fruit must be separated from the others. Corrugated paper or newspaper is folded into long sections approximately 2½ in (7 cm) deep and stapled to an adjoining length to make individual storage pockets for the fruits.*

BELOW: *Late summer and autumn are the best times for collecting wild fungi. Take care to identify them correctly and pick only good specimens. Clean them well with a fungi knife, brush off any moss and cut away the dirt. The larger varieties such as cèpes can be sliced and dried slowly in a warm place over a few days. When fully dry, store them in an airtight container.*

ABOVE: *At the end of the summer a large number of unripened green tomatoes are always left on the vine. Along with yellow raisins, they are one of the staple ingredients of many chutney recipes. Other late summer and autumn fruits such as zucchini and apples can also be used up in this way.*

CUT PAPER SHELF EDGING

THE SIMPLEST PROJECTS are often the most satisfying ones. This charming variation of the traditional technique of making paper shelf edging is a typical example. The application of this craft technique can be found all over the world and many different types of papers are used, from newspapers to doilies. It probably originated as a peasant craft – an inventive and inexpensive way of adding decoration to the home. Long sections could be used on a kitchen dresser; here subtly colored handmade paper has been used to decorate a small corner cupboard. Because it is so quick and easy to do, both the style and the color can be changed whenever you wish.

YOU WILL NEED

Sheet of pale mauve handmade paper
(size depends on the length
of the shelf to be decorated)

Sheet of natural colored
handmade paper

Scissors

Template
(see page 188)

Pencil and ruler

Pinking shears

Hole punches in two sizes

Embossed upholstery tacks,
for attaching to the shelf

1 Cut strips of pale mauve paper 3¼ in (8 cm) wide from the long side of the paper sheet and rule a line 1¼ in (3 cm) down from one edge. Place the template against this line and draw around with the pencil. Repeat until the pattern is drawn all the way along the line.

3 First use the larger hole punch to make a central hole in each scallop. Then, using the smaller hole punch, make a series of holes along the edge of the points and scallops. To fix onto your shelves, cut a strip of the natural paper approximately ¾ in (1.5 cm) and trim one edge with pinking shears. Place the straight edge directly over the straight edge of the mauve paper, hold the double thickness against the shelf edge and fix in place by pushing in the upholstery tacks at even intervals.

2 Carefully cut out around these lines using the pinking shears. It is easier to hold the patterned edge away from you and hold the pinking shears under the paper; you will need to turn the paper slightly to help make a neat zigzagged edge.

Jams and Preserves

LEFT: *For successful jam making it is essential to weigh your ingredients carefully and have all your equipment prepared in advance. A general rule is to use the same quantity of sugar as of fruit. When using pitted fruit, crack a few of the pits in order to release the pectin to help the jam set. Remove the pits before potting the jam.*

Choose or pick 4 lb (1.8 kg) of slightly underripe plums. Remove stalks and any bruised parts, then cut the plums into halves, reserving the pits. Place the fruit and ¾ pint (450 ml) water in a pan with 6 bruised cardamom pods and simmer gently for 15 minutes or until the fruit is tender. Crack about 20 pits and remove the kernels to add to the jam later. Add 4 lb (1.8 kg) granulated sugar to the fruit and stir over a low heat until dissolved. Bring to a boil and cook rapidly until setting point is reached after approximately 15 minutes. When ready, remove from heat, add the reserved kernels, skim and pour into clean, warm jars. Cover and seal while hot.

RIGHT: *Only firm, freshly gathered unblemished fruit should be used for making jam. Damson plums can be a little bitter to eat fresh from the tree, but they make an excellent jam.*

LEFT: *Add the subtle flavor of the scented geranium to crabapple jelly by setting a washed and dried leaf at the bottom of the jar before you strain in the freshly made jelly. As well as imparting its unusual fragrance, it makes a decorative feature in the transparent preserve.*

Wash and pick over 4 lb (1.8 kg) crabapples, discarding any that are bruised or rotten. Cut the apples into quarters and place in a stainless steel pan with 1¾ pints (1 liter) water and simmer gently until the fruit is soft and pulpy. Strain for a considerable time through a scalded jelly bag or a clean linen cloth — you need to be patient and avoid squeezing the bag or the resulting jelly will be cloudy. Measure the juice back into the saucepan and for every 1 pint (600 ml) liquid, add 1 lb (450 g) sugar. Stir over low heat to dissolve the sugar, then boil for about 15 minutes to reach setting point. Remove from the heat, cool slightly and skim before pouring into clean, warm jars, into the base of which has been placed a washed scented geranium leaf. Cover and seal while hot. Makes a little more than 4 lbs (2 kg).

RIGHT: *If you only make a few jars of jam at a time, you might like to paint some special watercolor labels to attach to the jars with matching colored ribbons. Cut out some rectangles of watercolor paper and paint the images of fruit. You will be surprised at how much more you know about the form of the fruit and the construction of the plant after this pleasurable activity.*

SEED STORAGE BOX

THIS USEFUL LITTLE storage box has been decorated with stenciled images of fern leaves, which have been gathered from the summer garden and pressed within the pages of a large book to preserve and flatten them. This charming method of decoration can also be applied on a much larger scale. For example, a tray to serve tea in the garden would make an ideal subject or, if you become very skillful, you may like to try decorating a kitchen cupboard.

YOU WILL NEED

Cardboard storage box
approximately 8¼ × 5¼ in
(21 × 13.5 cm) with a depth
of 3¼ in (8 cm)

Spray paint in green, brown
and yellow

Paper to protect work surface

Assortment of pressed fern leaves

Adjustable spray mount

Scissors

1 Spray green paint evenly over the box. Remember to cover your work surface with scrap paper and work outside or in a well-ventilated room.

2 Speckle the green base with the yellow and a little brown paint, creating a broken speckled finish that mimics the color of the ferns. To make the spray splutter to create this effect, press the button on the can very lightly.

3 Select the ferns that you intend to use and cut them to fit the lid and the sides of the box. Spray the backs with the adjustable adhesive (working in a well-ventilated place) and position them on the surface of the lid.

4 Spray brown paint over the ferns and allow to dry. Leave the sides of the lid unsprayed as a contrast. Repeat on all four sides of the box and allow to dry.

5 When the paint has dried, gently pull the ferns away to reveal their perfect image.

Preserving and Drying Flowers

THE KEY TO DRYING FLOWERS successfully is choosing the right moment to pick them – ideally a clear, sunny morning after the dew has evaporated. Choose the best, making sure the blooms are well shaped, blemish-free and not too open. Dry flowers as soon as possible after picking.

AIR DRYING

The simplest way of preserving flowers is air drying – a method suitable for many varieties and best for large quantities. Harvest flowers with stems as long as possible and strip large, untidy leaves from the stems. Gather smaller flowers into bunches; hang large blooms individually. Fasten each bunch 1 in (2.5 cm) from the stem ends with a rubber band – the stems shrink as they dry. To reduce the effects of dust or excessive light, cover each bunch with a paper bag and tie the open end of the bag around the stems.

Choose a warm place such as an airing cupboard or near hot pipes in a well-ventilated room and position flowers away from bright light. Good air circulation ensures that flowers dry quickly and keep their color. When ready, flowers feel dry and crisp with firm stems.

WATER DRYING

Flowers such as hydrangeas and gypsophila dry better standing upright in a vase containing about 2 in (5 cm) of water. It is essential to pick hydrangeas at just the right time for guaranteed success and this might involve some trial and error before you get it right. The florets should be hard and mature and not fully open. Place the container in a warm area out of direct sunlight. As the water slowly evaporates, the flowers dry.

ABOVE: *Dyed dried flowers take on a wonderful brilliance when sharp contrasting colors are used together. Use a florists' foam wreath base and simply push the flower stems into the foam all around the circle, mixing oak leaves, sunflowers and poppy seedheads in bright shades and natural zinnias in fabulous pinks and reds.*

RIGHT: *Lavender is easy to dry and has a practical as well as decorative use when preserved. The dried flowers can fill sachets for the linen cupboard to scent the linens and keep moths at bay. Bundles of lavender can be displayed quite simply when tightly packed into baskets or terra-cotta pots.*

LEFT: *Dahlias with double flowers and broad petals can be dried successfully. Dry the flower heads in a dimly lit room to help retain their vibrant colors and store them away from daylight to preserve their beauty until they are needed. Horizontally suspended lengths of wire mesh can be used to support the freshly picked dahlias as they dry.*

ABOVE: *Dried mop-head hydrangeas come in a beautiful array of shades, from blues and lavenders to burnished reds and pinks. Used alone, you will only need half a dozen plump flower heads to fill a large bowl or tureen for a lush display.*

DESICCANTS

Desiccants such as silica gel, borax or sand can be used to absorb the water from flowers and leaves. This is a useful method for delicate flower heads, including peonies, anemones, lilacs, roses and pansies. Silica gel (available from florist suppliers) is a powdery substance that quickly absorbs moisture and can be used again and again if it is occasionally dried out in the oven. Drying should be done in airtight containers.

Place flowers face up in the gel (except for daisies, zinnias and gerbera, which are dried face down). Press gently into the gel and make sure the insides of the flowers are well covered. Shake the gel gently over the blossom. Check the flowers each day until they turn dry (but not brittle). Thin-petaled flowers take 2–3 days to dry, fleshy-headed flowers 5–7 days.

FLOWERS IDEAL FOR DRYING

Peonies - Choose double varieties for drying as single flowers fall apart after picking. Avoid white peonies, as they go brown as they dry

Lavender - Pick the flower at its bluest, when the flower is mature but not out. Cut an early crop and a second flourish of flowers in early autumn can result.

Zinnias - Dry flower heads in silica gel to retain their shape and color. Place them in water for a while after picking so the flowers become bigger and then dry.

Roses - Many types of roses can be dried successfully, although single varieties fall apart after picking. Choose scented varieties for fragrant displays.

Hydrangea - Mop-head *hortensia* hydrangeas are best for drying. The florets must be hard and mature when they are picked.

DRAWSTRING HERB BAGS

HOMEGROWN HERBS harvested from the garden can be dried and stored for use in the kitchen. Instead of crumbling them into glass jars and containers, small linen sacks make a more decorative alternative. Hang them on pegs in the larder or, for tisanes and infusions, beside the kettle. Scraps and oddments of old linen can be turned into homespun bags to keep the herbs dust-free, each one embroidered with the name of the herb worked in chain stitch. Here we have used the Latin names for herbs.

YOU WILL NEED

A remnant of linen 20 × 13½ in (50 × 34 cm) – this makes a bag measuring 12¼ × 8½ in (31 × 22 cm)

Template (see page 188)

Pencil

Dressmakers' tracing paper

Soft cotton embroidery thread

Embroidery needle

Scissors

Sewing thread

Pins

27½ in (70 cm) cord

1 *Cut the fabric in half to make two rectangles 10 × 13½ in (25 × 34 cm). Write the herb name onto paper so it will fit within one of the fabric pieces for the bag front, then pin the paper in position on the fabric with a layer of tracing paper between so the carbon faces the right side of the fabric. Draw over the herb name, pressing down hard to transfer the word onto the fabric. Embroider the herb name with a continuous line of chain stitch.*

2 *Turn under and press ¾ in (15 mm) to the wrong side on the sides and base edges of the front and back pieces, mitering the bottom corners. Turn under the top edge in the same way, pin and stitch in place. With wrong sides facing, pin the front of the bag to the back, matching seams, and join together along the sides and base sewing in ⅝ in (12 mm) in from the edges.*

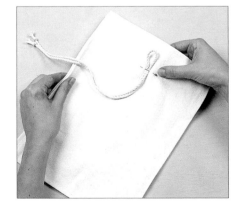

3 *Knot each end of the cord and cut to make small tassels. Fold the cord in half and pin to the center of the bag back 2½ in (6 cm) down from the top and 1½ in (4 cm) down from the centerfold of the cord, so it forms a hanging loop. Stitch in place.*

LINEN SACHET

AROMATIC LAVENDER and freshly laundered linens make a classic combination. This linen sachet is in the form of a flat pillow that can nestle between piles of clean sheets in the linen cupboard, keeping them smelling sweet. The herb passes its unmistakable aroma to the surrounding fabrics and also acts as a repellent to moths and insects. Dried lavender keeps its scent for a long time, but a shake now and again helps to release more oils and renew the smell. A fine calico sachet contains the dried flowers and fits inside the outer pillowcase, so it is easily replaced when the bouquet starts to fade.

YOU WILL NEED

A piece of fine calico
16 × 24 in (40 × 60 cm)

6 oz (180 g) dried lavender

5 small buttons

Sewing thread

Scissors

16 in (40 cm) of linen,
36 in (90 cm) wide

Pins

16 in (40 cm) length of ribbon,
2¾ in (7 cm) wide

48 in (1.2 m) length of ribbon,
¾ in (1 cm) wide

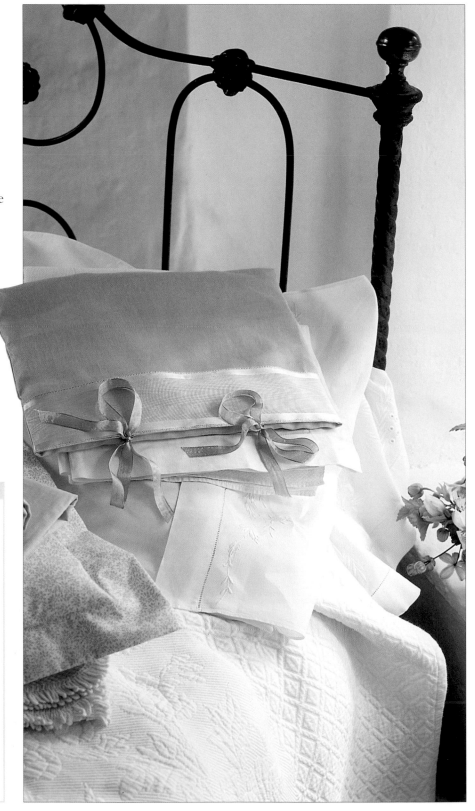

1 For the sachet, cut two rectangles of calico, each 15 × 11½ in (38 × 29 cm). Place the rectangles right sides facing and with matching edges, and stitch around the four sides, taking ¾ in (1.5 cm) seams. Leave a gap in one side 4 in (10 cm) long. Trim the seams and turn to right side.

2 Fill the sachet loosely with dried lavender and slip stitch the gap to keep the lavender secure inside the bag. Arrange the lavender evenly within the bag and lay it flat. Place the five buttons evenly on the bag and sew them in place, stitching through all thicknesses to help hold the lavender in place.

3 Cut a rectangle of linen 24½ × 15 in (62.5 × 38 cm). Turn under and press ½ in (1 cm) to the right side along one short edge. Cut the fine ribbon into four equal lengths and pin two lengths to the folded edge, 4½ in (11 cm) in from the edge with ribbon ends level with edge of the inside fold.

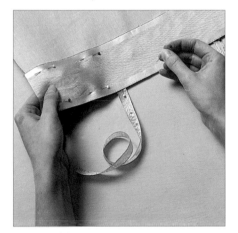

5 Turn and stitch a hem of ½ in (1 cm) then ¾ in (1.5 cm) along the opposite short edge, turning the hem to the wrong side. With right sides facing, fold the rectangle to bring the ribboned edge of the rectangle to within 3¾ in (8 cm) of the opposite hemmed edge, matching side edges.

4 Place the length of wide ribbon on the right side of the rectangle so the outer edge of the ribbon matches the folded edge of the fabric and trim the ends level with the sides. Pin and tack, then stitch close to the edges of the ribbon.

6 Fold the hemmed edge 3¾ in (8 cm) over the ribbon edge, matching side edges to form the "pillowcase." Pin and stitch sides, taking ¾ in (1.5 cm) seams. Trim seams, turn right sides out and press. Fold over one end of each remaining length of narrow ribbon and stitch inside the folded edge of the case to correspond with the ties on the ribboned edge. Place the sachet inside the case and tie the ribbons in bows.

QUINCES

THIS FRAGRANT FRUIT appears in stores in the autumn, at about the same time as pomegranates, and is a great favorite of the southern and eastern Mediterranean, where it grows in abundance on small trees. Looking like a variety of yellow knobbly pear, it is extremely hard even when ripe, although it imparts a perfumed scent that gives a clue to its culinary flavor.

Quinces are made into jam and syrup in Iran and Greece, and in Spain into a "cheese" called *membrillo*, which is eaten as a sweet with real cheese, usually manchego. You will need to add a lot of sugar to bring out the flavor of quinces, so one of the best recipes is to poach them in halves in quince syrup and serve with a saffron ice cream.

QUINCE "CHEESE"

3¼ lb (1½ kg) quinces
1 lb (450 g) sugar to each 1 lb (450 g)
of pulp
Superfine sugar, for dredging

Wash, peel, core and chop the quinces into pieces. Put them in a pan with the cores and the peel, just cover with water and simmer gently for half an hour until really soft. Push the fruit through a sieve to remove any seeds or peel and weigh the resulting pulp. Return it to the pan with the appropriate amount of sugar. Stir over low heat until the sugar has dissolved, then boil gently until the mixture darkens and thickens considerably and comes away from the sides of the pan. Remove from the heat and pour onto a sheet of baking parchment placed on a cold, flat surface. Leave to set overnight, then cut into squares. To serve as sweets, dredge them individually with superfine sugar.

BAKED SPICED QUINCE

1 lemon
6 quinces
6 cardamom pods
6 cloves
13 fl oz (375 ml) sweet white wine
3 oz (75 g) superfine sugar

Pre-heat the oven to 325°F (160°C). Pare thin strips off the lemon rind using a sharp potato peeler and set aside. Cut the lemons in quarters. Rub the down from the skins of the quinces, then cut the fruit into quarters, removing the core. Rub the cut sides of the quinces with the lemon and place them skin side down in an enamel dish. Squeeze the remaining lemon juice over the fruit. Bruise the cardamoms until they split. Sprinkle the cardamoms, cloves and lemon zest over the quinces. Pour over the wine and sprinkle with the sugar. Bake in the oven for two hours by which time the quinces will have taken on a lovely rosy pink color. Serve warm or cold with crème fraîche.

BLACKBERRY BLANKET

AT THIS TIME OF YEAR blackberries can be gathered and bottled and preserved for the months to come. Continue the autumnal theme by making this cozy blanket – just what we need when the nights are turning colder and longer.

Adding the blackberry embellishment to a plain blanket transforms it from the practical to something extraordinary that can be used to decorate the bed or sofa or just to wear, wrapped around yourself while watching television. Good quality woolen blankets can be very expensive, so look for old cream-colored blankets in good condition that can be dyed gorgeous colors. Decorate with ribbon or a rich velvet border to make something truly unique.

YOU WILL NEED

A blanket

Rickrack braid, enough to run twice around all four sides of the blanket

Ribbon, enough to run once around all four sides of the blanket

Small bobble braid

Short lengths of velvet ribbon, ¾ in (1 cm) wide

Scissors

Sewing thread

Needle

1 Tack the rickrack braid along both sides of the ribbon.

2 Pin the ribbon to the sides of the blanket 1¼ in (3 cm) in from the edge, folding the corners to miter them where they turn. Tack the ribbon in place, then machine-stitch close to both edges. Slip-stitch the mitered corners together.

3 Cut the bobble braid into lengths of approximately 17 bobbles and plan where each blackberry will be placed, scattered over the blanket in a random way. Hand-stitch the braid length to the blanket to form a blackberry shape, winding the braid back on itself where necessary and hiding the braid edging underneath the bobbles.

4 Cut the velvet ribbon into 10 in (25 cm) lengths. Take one length and pleat it four times to make a blackberry stalk, then hand-stitch it together to secure the folds at one end. Place the stalk on the top of the blackberry and stitch in place. Work the other blackberries in the same way to complete the throw.

FLAVORED OILS AND VINEGARS

O NE OF THE SIMPLEST and most effective culinary treats is to make your own flavored oils and vinegars. These seem to be unreasonably expensive to buy when you consider that the making of them is so speedy. A flavored or spicy oil adds interest to cooking and they are particularly useful for making interesting varieties of salad dressings. You can be quite inventive when choosing your flavors – after all it is you who will be using them.

Use only the best ingredients – choose fresh herbs such as tarragon or coriander, unblemished fruit and spices, quality vinegars and virgin olive oil. For a piquant flavor, infuse a red chili and a couple of garlic cloves in the oil; for a more Mediterranean style add a few sprigs of rosemary to the bottle before pouring over the oil. Blackberries or raspberries add a wonderful fruity tang to vinegar and give it a strong color.

Both the oils and the vinegars need to be stored for about four weeks before use in order to intensify the flavor. Decanted into pretty bottles and labeled, they also make very welcome gifts for avid cooks.

ROASTED WHOLE GARLIC IN OLIVE OIL

Place a whole garlic in a roasting pan and drizzle with a little olive oil and cook in an oven preheated to 375°F (190°C) for about 20 minutes. Allow to cool slightly, then place in the bottom of a wide-topped jar. Fill the jar with extra virgin olive oil and seal with a matching lid or closely fitting cork. Store for about four weeks before use to allow the garlic to infuse its flavor into the oil.

CHILI OIL

Peel and bruise a couple of large garlic cloves and place at the bottom of clean glass bottle. Select an unblemished red chili, stem intact and with a satisfying shape, and place upright in the bottle alongside the garlic. Pour over some extra virgin olive oil and firmly cork the bottle. After four weeks, serve with ciabatta bread, ground sea salt and freshly milled black pepper.

WINTER

Entertaining for Friends

WITH CHRISTMAS as the main focal point of the winter months, this is the time for entertaining, when friends and family celebrate the warmth and goodwill of the season. The main Christmas feast is often the high point of the whole celebration, when the family comes together to enjoy an especially lavish meal. As well as the preparation and planning involved with the food, it is an opportunity to decorate the table to create a special mood and a memorable occasion. Choosing a cool metallic color scheme gives a frosty shimmer to the proceedings, making a welcome change from a more traditional red and green color scheme.

Place Settings

RIGHT: *For an unusual after-dinner treat, serve little iced almond paste cakes as petits fours. In southern France they are called calissons and are traditionally made from ground almonds and crushed glacé melon. You can make a homemade version from rolled marzipan cut into shapes and covered with a fine coating of royal icing. A Provençal Christmas tradition is to serve a selection of 13 desserts that are left on the table from Christmas Eve until Twelfth Night, including fresh raisins and prunes, glacé cherries, nougat made with honey and almonds and calissons.*

ABOVE: *Frayed strips of metallic organdy can be used to tie up each napkin and add a candlelight shimmer to the dinner table. Cut the fabric into strips approximately 31 in (80 cm) long and 3¼ in (8 cm) wide, then pull away the threads along all four edges to a depth of ½ in (1.5 cm). Roll the napkins loosely, then tie in place with the organdy strip, loosely tied in a knot that can be slipped off the napkin by each diner.*

LEFT: Votive candles on the table make the cutlery and glassware glint in a special way, worthy of the occasion. Look for small clear glass candleholders that will let the light glow through, crazed glass containers that really catch the candlelight, colored glass mosaics or beaded candleholders for the best effects.

RIGHT: We all love to receive gifts, so place an exquisitely wrapped parcel at each place setting with the name of its intended recipient written on each one to indicate the seating plan. It might be a tiny box of chocolates or something more extravagant for a special occasion.

ABOVE: To continue the subtle metallic color theme, cakeboards make simple placemats and come in lots of different shapes and sizes. A fine coating of colored metallic spray paint will tint the silver textured foil and make it look far grander than its original use intended. Buy square, rectangular or oblong boards that are large enough to show underneath a large dinner plate and have space to accommodate cutlery and a wine glass.

WINTER HOUSEPLANTS

THE TRADITIONAL winter or festive plants such as cyclamens, capsicums and poinsettias are all rather too familiar now. It is quite possible to make far more original tabletop displays by combining an unusual plant with a specially decorated pot.

The shape and restrained color of the small woody evergreen heather make a wonderful combination with the partly gilded galvanized pot. Wide stripes have been painted with gold size, and when it is sticky, or almost dry, the strips of silver or aluminum leaf have been applied. As the heather is a hardy perennial it will be quite happy growing outside in the garden after Christmas, and the pot can continue to be used as a vase for flowers.

This idea could easily be adapted to become a striking centerpiece for a dining table by using shorter containers and smaller plants.

METALLIC TABLE RUNNER

TABLE RUNNER can be used to make a plain tablecloth look spectacular. If a large table is being set for many guests you can use a plain cotton sheet to cover the table right down to the ground, then add a table runner along the center of the table to lift the overall appearance. It also provides a unified look when all the plates, cutlery and glassware are placed on the table.

Metallic organdy has a luxurious quality and is available in an exquisite range of colors. Fringed bands of contrasting organdy are simply stitched in place across the width of the runner, the fringed edges used for decoration and texture. The runner shown here measures approximately 3 yds × 22½ in (280 × 57 cm), but you can adjust the size to fit your table.

YOU WILL NEED

1½ yds (1.40 m) metallic organdy, 45 in (112 cm) wide, in the main color

20 in (50 cm) in each of three other colors of metallic organdy

Tape measure

Scissors and pins

Sewing thread

7½ yds (7 m) fringed braid

1 Cut the main fabric in half lengthways to make two strips 1½ yds (1.4 m) long and 22 in (56 cm) wide. Join the strips together to make one long strip by overlapping two ends by ½ in (1.5 cm) and sewing with the sewing machine using a zigzag stitch. Cut six strips 3¼ in (8 cm) wide and 19 in (48 cm) long out of the two of the contrasting fabrics and seven strips out of the third color. Fringe the edges on all four sides of each strips to a depth of ½ in (1.5 cm).

2 Starting with the color with seven strips, pin a strip centrally across the width to the right side of the runner and 4 in (10 cm) away from one end of the runner. Stitch in place with a machine zigzag stitch along all sides of the strip. Pin and stitch the other strips in place, positioning them 2½ in (6 cm) apart and following the same color sequence along the length of the runner. The final strip should be the same color as the first one.

3 Pin the braid along all four edges of the runner then stitch it in place to finish. Press the runner carefully with a cool iron.

EMBROIDERED TABLE MATS

MBROIDERY adds a touch of class to simple table mats. The crown motifs are worked in cross-stitch and are quick to complete. Scrap canvas is used to provide the regular grid needed to keep the stitches even. The canvas comes in gauges measured by threads to the inch, and the gauge will determine the finished size of the motif.

Using scrap canvas means that cross-stitch can be worked onto any fabric, not just an even weave type, and the embroidery can be positioned at any angle. The finished mat measures $16\frac{1}{4} \times 2\frac{1}{4}$ in (41×31 cm).

YOU WILL NEED

Piece of scrap canvas
$4\frac{3}{4} \times 3\frac{1}{2}$ in (12×9 cm),
8.5 threads per 1 in (2.5 cm)

Piece of cotton fabric 44×34 cm
($17\frac{1}{4} \times 13\frac{1}{4}$ in) for each table mat

Pins and crewel needle, size 7

Sewing thread and needle

Stranded cotton embroidery thread

Scissors

Tape measure

Backing fabric and interlining,
cut to the same dimensions as
the main fabric

Scraps of metallic organdy
for binding

1 Pin the scrap of canvas to the right side of the mat front fabric, placing it diagonally across the bottom left-hand corner. Tack it in place, remove the pins, then tack guidelines across the canvas following the center threads so the lines cross at the center point of the canvas.

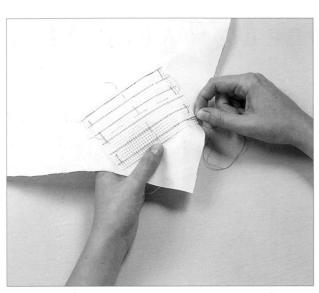

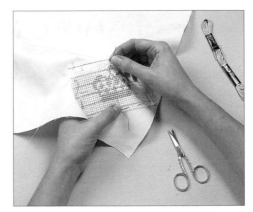

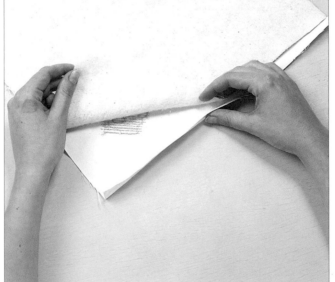

2 Work the cross-stitch motif following the chart shown on page 190, using three strands of thread throughout and placing the motif centrally on the canvas, following the guidelines.

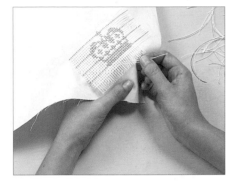

3 Remove the tacking and guidelines, then remove the waste canvas by pulling away the warp and weft threads one by one. Keep the threads close to the fabric as they are pulled out from beneath the stitches so the cross-stitches are not stretched.

4 Turn under and press to the wrong side the ½ in (1.5 cm) seam allowance along both short edges of the mat front. Trim the ½ in (1.5 cm) seam allowance from both short edges of the interlining and place it on the wrong side of the mat front, matching long edges and folding the turnings on the front over the interlining.

5 Turn under the seam allowance to the wrong side on both short edges of the mat backing fabric. With right sides facing, pin the backing to the front and stitch down the long edges, taking ½ in (1.5 cm) seams. Trim the seams neatly, turn to the right side and press.

6 Cut two strips of metallic organdy 13¼ in (34 cm) long and 3¼ in (8 cm) wide. Pin a strip of organdy to the right side of one of the short edges of the mat front and stitch ¾ in (2 cm) in from the edge. To bind the edges, turn the organdy to the wrong side over the end of the mat and fold under ¾ in (2 cm) of the organdy on the wrong side. Fold the organdy ends in at the sides underneath the mat and slip-stitch in place. Bind the other end in the same way.

CHRISTMAS CRACKERS

RACKERS CAN BE extremely expensive to buy at Christmas considering they are so easy to make. One of the biggest advantages of making your own is that you can enhance or match your chosen table setting theme and add a small personalized present to each cracker. The combination of the subtly striped hand-printed paper used for the body of the cracker and the stunning metallic paper used to make the crown decorations is an unusual and effective one.

1 Cut the striped paper into a rectangle measuring 6½ × 15 in (16.5 × 38 cm) — the paper needs to be wide enough to wrap all around the cardboard tube with some overlap. Roll it around the tube and stick in place with the paper glue.

YOU WILL NEED

Four sheets of striped wrapping paper (such as pink, blue, purple and orange stripes on black)

Ruler

Four cardboard tubes, 4 in (10 cm) long and 2 in (5 cm) wide

Scissors

Paper glue

Cracker snappers and small gifts

Short lengths of coordinating rayon ribbons

Scraps of metallic paper in orange, green, red and pink

Template (see page 188)

Small scissors

Small piece of scrap cardboard

Sewing tracing wheel

2 Thread the cracker snapper into the open tube and insert a little gift. Pinch the paper together where it reaches the end of the tube and tie each end in place with a matching length of ribbon.

3 Cut out the crown shapes from the colored metallic paper using the template as a guide. Turn over so that the right side is placed facedown on the piece of cardboard and roll the tracing wheel firmly over the back to create the raised bobbly pattern on the shiny side.

4 Stick the finished crown onto the central part of the cracker at a slight angle using the paper glue.

Decorating the Christmas Tree

O NE OF THE MOST exciting parts of the Christmas festivities is decorating the tree. In some traditional countries, the tree is not cut from the forest until Christmas Eve. It is carried back home, often through the snow, and set down in the center of the house, imparting its wonderful foresty smell. Some households like to invent a new style each Christmas, while others prefer to bring out all the old favorite decorations. Whatever your choice, adorning the tree with all its pagan overtones is a particularly enjoyable part of Christmas, especially for children who really do believe in magic.

SILVER CHRISTMAS BIRD

A REALLY SPLENDID Christmas tree needs to be topped with a shining star, an elegant angel or, as in this case, a glittering bird. These handmade tree decorations become family treasures, to be passed down from one generation to the next and carefully stored away each year as the tree is dismantled. This bird is made from aluminum foil (thicker than the kitchen variety) and the raised pattern is created using a ballpoint pen and a tracing wheel of the kind usually used in sewing.

YOU WILL NEED

Roll of extra heavy aluminum foil

Small scissors

Template (see page 188)

Transparent tape

Wad of tissue paper

Dried-up ballpoint pen

Double-sided tape

Sewing tracing wheel

1 Cut out two pieces of the aluminum foil, each slightly larger than the template. Working on one at a time, stick the template on to the metal using the transparent tape. Place on the wad of tissue paper and draw around the template with the ballpoint pen, pressing firmly to transfer the design. Remove the template, reverse it and cut another from the second piece of metal. You should now have two halves of the bird.

2 Cut out both sides of the bird and lay one on the wad of tissue. Use the tracing wheel to make an outline around the shape. Make a double line at the top of the wing. Use the ballpoint pen to make four stars in each scalloped shape at the top of the wing.

4 Delineate the beak and mark the neck as shown. Mark an arc on the breast area with a double line using the tracing wheel and then make a pattern of crossed lines. Change to the ballpoint pen and draw dots in each square. Repeat all this on the other side of the bird, remembering that when you fit the two halves together the raised pattern must appear on the outside of each half.

3 Use the tracing wheel to mark three vertical lines on the wing. Make a similar pattern on the tail and make a star for the eye.

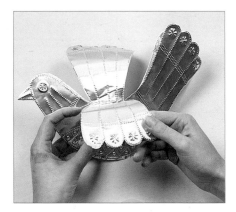

5 Stick the two halves of the bird together using strips of double-sided tape. You will need to stick all areas except the wings. To create the three dimensional effect, bend each wing gently away from each other. To store the bird, simply flatten the wings together.

LEAFY GARLAND

THIS LUSTROUS COPPER leaf garland, surprisingly inexpensive and quick to make, will add elegance and style to your Christmas tree. Here the small leaves are cut in the shape of the willow and the oak and are threaded together and interspaced with glittering glass beads, although any old beads, perhaps left over from another project, would do equally well. The metal foil is soft thin copper and is available from specialist craft suppliers. If you have difficulty finding the foil, try using disposable aluminum food containers or pie dishes. The raised dotted lines delineating the leaf veins are simply made using a sewing tracing wheel.

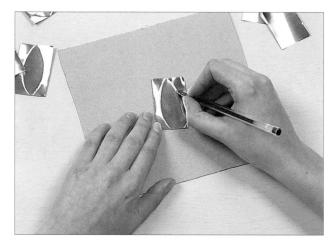

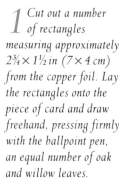

1 Cut out a number of rectangles measuring approximately 2¾ × 1½ in (7 × 4 cm) from the copper foil. Lay the rectangles onto the piece of card and draw freehand, pressing firmly with the ballpoint pen, an equal number of oak and willow leaves.

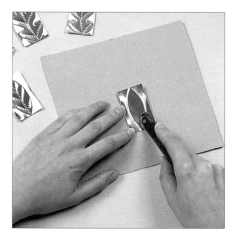

2 Using the tracing wheel and pressing firmly, roll the central vein and add the radiating lines. You are now working on the back of the leaf, the raised bobbly line created with the tracing wheel will appear on the front of the leaf.

3 Using the small scissors, cut neatly around the perimeter of the leaf just outside the outline marked with the ballpoint pen. Place the cut-out leaf back on the card and use the bradawl to pierce a small hole at the base and top end. Repeat on each leaf.

YOU WILL NEED

Roll of copper foil

Ruler

Dried-up ballpoint pen

Sewing tracing wheel

Small scissors

Fine wire

Bradawl

Assortment of glass beads

Piece of card as yielding surface

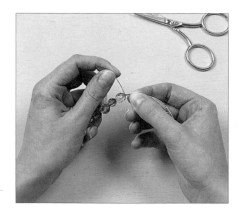

4 Cut a 4 in (10 cm) length of the fine wire and twist and secure one end through the pierced hole at the base or top of a leaf, then thread on five beads and pass the remaining wire through the hole at the end of the next leaf (use one oak leaf, followed by a willow leaf, then another oak leaf). Twist the wire around on itself and snip off the excess. Continue threading the garland together in this manner.

CORRUGATED PAPER BIRDS

THIS EXOTIC FLOCK of brightly colored birds looks as if it has landed on the deep green branches of the Christmas tree. Arranged with lengths of twisted duotone crepe paper to make garlands, they look quite stunning and are just the thing to brighten up the dull days of mid-winter. Little fans of folded crepe paper are slotted through corrugated card bodies and opened out to create the three-dimensional effect. Duotone crepe paper is perfect for this project — it is made by bonding two contrasting colors together. If you cannot find this paper, simply fold a double layer of contrasting crepe papers to create a similar effect.

YOU WILL NEED

Sheet each of green and purple finely corrugated cardboard (microboard)

Template (see page 190)

Pen

Scissors

Craft knife

Cutting mat

Hole punch

White glue

Two rolls of duotone crepe paper in orange/yellow and pink/red

Paper clips

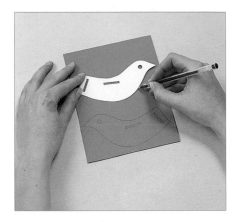

1 Cut out a piece of the green cardboard large enough to fit the bird template twice. Hold the template in place on the smooth side of the card and draw around it twice to make two opposite halves (turn the template over so the beak and tail are pointing in opposite direction for the second half).

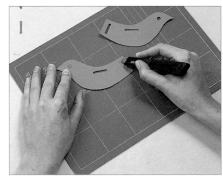

2 Cut out the bird shapes and use the craft knife and cutting mat to cut out the slots indicated on the template. Make the hole for the eye with the hole punch.

3 Stick the two halves of the bird together, corrugated sides out, using the white glue. Take care not to use too much glue to avoid it spreading out onto the corrugated side of the card.

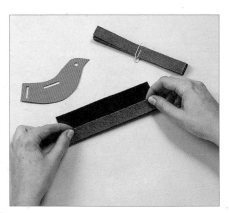

4 Cut out two pieces of duotone crepe paper 6 in (15 cm) square and fold accordian-style into a fan. Each fold should be slightly narrower than the slots in the body and the tail. Hold together with a paper clip in the middle.

5 Push the first fan through the body slot, making sure that equal amounts protrude each side. Bend the fan in half , opening it out above the body, and stick the two sides together at the top. Hold with a paper clip at the top until the glue is dry. Repeat the same process with the tail fan to finish the bird.

Decorating the Tree

RIGHT: *Chocolate money is usually tantalizingly suspended in little woven metal bags from branches of the Christmas tree. Although the method of stringing them onto gold cord to make garlands means that it is easier for inquisitive fingers secretly to remove one or two, the overall effect is very beautiful. Each coin has simply been glued onto the cord — it is quickest to use a glue gun.*

BELOW: *These vibrantly colored necklaces of fresh cranberries and tiny squares of orange peel are simple enough for children to make. The deep reds of the cranberries and the scent of the orange peel as it dries make this a special combination.*

ABOVE: *Traditional Christmas cookies, which are baked in great anticipation of the festive days to come, are great favorites. Bake your cookies with a hole in the middle so that a ribbon can be threaded through to hang on the tree.*

ABOVE: *Here is a miniature version of the traditional pomander. Tiny kumquats and limes are quartered with cloves and wrapped with narrow satin ribbon, ready to decorate the tree. An unribbonned selection would look lovely displayed in a basket or colored china bowl.*

RIGHT: *If the chocolate money is for children, then these superior chocolate bars are for adults. Really good chocolate gives off an inviting fragrance. Buy little bars from a specialty shop and suspend them in the tree with coordinating taffeta ribbon*

Decorating the Home

CHRISTMAS REALLY IS THE TIME to go to town and decorate the house. It could simply be a matter of pinning festive greeting cards onto ribbons to be garlanded around the room, or it might be a more elaborate affair involving shopping for special materials to concoct wonderful creations.

Holly and mistletoe have been prized for centuries for their ability to produce their fruits in winter when all else is bare. To the Romans, holly signified good health in the year ahead and renewal of life. For the Druids it was mistletoe that held a special place and was thought to protect the home and its occupants. Whether we make decorations to embellish our homes or buy them ready-made, we are following an age-old tradition that has always held a special magic.

GILDED CANDLES

FOR A SPECIAL festive occasion, try decorating white church candles with a layer of gold leaf. It is not necessary to use the normal gold size as the fine gold leaf adheres beautifully to the surface of the wax when pressed and rubbed on with the fingers. This is easiest to do if the candle is at room temperature. The loosely drawn star pattern is simply made using the tip of a knife blade.

You may like to decorate a group of candles of different sizes with a variety of patterns. For the best effect, keep the designs simple, such as stripes and wavy lines. The same technique can be applied to colored candles so that a color will shine through the scratched away pattern. If the gold leaf does not cover the area, cut the leaves with sharp scissors into sections and apply patchwork-style using the method described here.

YOU WILL NEED

White church candles, approximately 3¼ in (8 cm) in diameter, 4¾ and 8 in (12 and 20 cm) high

A book of transfer gold leaf

Small kitchen knife

Wad of tissue paper or paper towels

1 Take one leaf of the gold and carefully lay it gold side down against the surface of the candle, with the tissue backing paper facing upward. Press very firmly and evenly with the fingers so that the gold adheres to the wax. You will be able to tell when the gold has stuck to the wax because you can see it pull away from its tissue backing.

2 Continue working all around the candle until the surface is covered. To protect the gilded surface, rest the candle on a wad of tissue paper. To make the star design draw four crossed lines with the tip of the knife blade — you do not need to cut into the wax, just lightly scrape the surface.

FLOWERS AND CANDLES

CANDLES INCORPORATED into flower arrangements draw attention to individual flowers and leaves when the candles are lit. You might especially want to use candles in an arrangement for Christmas, as candlelight goes hand in hand with the festivities. A good florist will be able to supply all the special materials needed. Never leave lit candles in a room unattended and extinguish the flames well before they reach the level of any foliage, especially if the arrangement includes dry and flammable materials.

ABOVE: *To make a garland, collect foliage that will survive for more than a few days in a warm room, such as trims from the Christmas tree, ivy with berries, rosemary and laurel. Cut the foliage into 6 in (15 cm) lengths. Bind the plant stems to a length of twine with florists' wire. Bunch the different kinds of foliage in alternating groups, pointing in one direction with the leaves of one group overlapping the stems of the previous one. Wedge tall candles in small bowls using pebbles or florists' foam to hold them steady and place them on the shelf, then arrange the garland around them. Place dried hydrangea flower heads along the length of the garland. Decorate with ribbon bows and Christmas baubles held in place with wires.*

RIGHT: *Making a flower arrangement in a terra-cotta pot couldn't be easier and the results look highly professional. Line the pot with a thick layer of polythene to make it waterproof, then push in a piece of florists' foam so it is wedged tightly and sits just above the pot's rim. Fill any gaps at the sides with smaller pieces of foam. Push a tall church candle into the foam so it is steady. Fill the container with water, allowing the foam to soak up the liquid. Arrange the foliage around the base of the candle to form the outline, then add flowers, arranging them in groups. Here eucalyptus stems form the basic shape of the arrangement, mixed with sprigs of hypericum berries, terra-cotta—colored roses and vivid lime-green chrysanthemums. They complement the color of the painted pot perfectly.*

LEFT: *It is important when making a table centerpiece with candles that the candles are held firmly, so using a pumpkin works particularly well. Choose a pumpkin with a flat base that will sit steadily on the table. Cut out three round holes with a knife and push a candle into each one. Make smaller holes into the flesh with a skewer to hold stems of deep brown cotinus leaves and ivy, filling the candle holes with water to keep the foliage fresh.*

LINOCUT LIMES

ONE OF THE MOST effective ways of making a lovely Christmas display, these pretty patterned citrus fruits look beautiful piled in a bowl where they can impart their tangy fragrance to the room. Limes have been used here but all citrus fruits are suitable.

The pattern is cut with a lino-cutting tool when the fruit is fresh. The cut away rind reveals a porous area of pith through which the moisture of the fruit gradually evaporates. The fruits eventually dry out and will last a long time, similar to pomanders. They could even be used as tree decorations.

YOU WILL NEED

Limes or other citrus fruit

Lino-cutting tool

Fine pen

1 To make stripes, use the lino-cutting tool to channel out thin lines from the top to the base of the lime as shown. The trick is not to cut too deeply so the tool will travel across the surface of the skin smoothly and evenly. Always push the tool away from you, and take care not to place your fingers in its path.

2 To make the spiral design, first draw the design onto the skin and then follow the lines with the cutting tool. As you become more experienced, you will probably not need to draw the design first and can simply cut the design freehand.

KUMQUATS AND LIMES

THIS STUNNING CONE of bright orange kumquats and vivid green baby limes makes an unusual sideboard display, with the vibrant citrus colors literally glowing in the soft Christmas candlelight and artfully reflected in the mirror set on the wall behind.

Each fruit has a short length of florists' wire threaded through one end. The two protruding ends of the wire are then twisted and pushed into a cone of dry florists' foam. The fruits have been arranged in tiers of contrasting color and the finished effect resembles the classic French croquembouche dessert, made with layers of cream puffs.

The same idea can easily be adapted to create a towering display of delicious sweets wrapped in glittering paper, assorted nuts with evergreen leaves or dried rosebuds.

CUT PAPER SHADE

THE DELICATE PAPER CUTOUT design of this professional looking lampshade belies the simplicity of its making. A pattern has been made from an existing paper lampshade and the partly cut motifs are easily created by using the templates provided. Once you become experienced at this unusual technique, you may wish to create your own individual designs. It is best to use white or natural-colored paper or parchment for this project as this helps to create a subtle range of tones when the lamp is lit. Some wire lampshade frames have connecting vertical sections, which are easier to work with.

YOU WILL NEED

Lampshade and frame

Sheet of ivory parchment-style paper large enough to accommodate the lampshade used as a pattern

Transparent tape

Sharp pencil

Scissors

Templates (see page 185)

Cutting mat

Craft knife

Strong glue

Clothespins

Masking tape (optional)

1 Remove the shade from an existing lampshade and open it out on parchment paper, securing it with tape. Draw around with pencil to transfer the outline; cut out.

2 Using the templates of the butterfly and moth, draw around them in pencil onto the paper, spacing them out equally along the curved shape.

3 Lay the paper on the cutting mat and use the craft knife to cut around the templates. Be extra careful always to leave a join so that part of the motif remains attached to the paper. For the butterfly, cut around the tips of the wings and antennae leaving the body, tail and head sections intact. For the flowers, cut around the petals, leaving a small section uncut where the petals join.

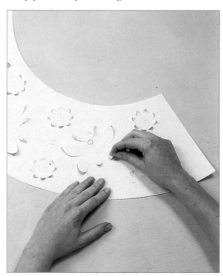

4 When you have finished cutting, curl up the wing tips, antennae and the flower petals with your fingers so that they stand away from the flat background.

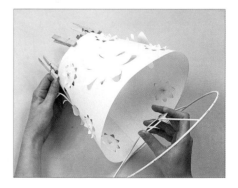

5 Roll the paper round on itself so it is exactly the same size as the original shade and glue along the join. You can use double-sided tape here if you find it easier. Slot the top section of the original frame in place and put a line of glue where the paper and wire touch. Hold in place with the clothespins and repeat with the base section. Allow the glue to dry. Neaten these edges if necessary by binding with masking tape.

GILDED CANDLESTICK

Tʜɪs ᴇʟᴇɢᴀɴᴛ, tall wooden candlestick has been decorated using a different gilding technique to the one shown on page 166. Instead of using gold leaf, the metal (in this instance, copper) has been mixed into a wax base to produce a fine powder. This makes it a particularly suitable method for gilding complicated surfaces such as the turned candlestick shown here or molded picture frames. It is an ideal project for transforming a tired and familiar household object.

Many people consider gilding a mysterious technique requiring a great deal of skill and experience. It is, of course, true that the more experience you have, the better the results, but in essence it is a simple technique with a glorious history that is available to all. This method of gilding with wax cream is a good way to begin this fascinating craft.

1 If the candlestick is not already primed, apply the white primer and allow to dry thoroughly. Next, apply two coats of pale pink paint and allow to dry. At this stage, you can sand the surface with very fine sandpaper to obtain a smooth finish, if you wish.

2 Apply the gilt cream on a rag and gently rub into the surface with a circular motion. Don't apply too much at a time as you need to obtain a broken finish where you can see the base color showing through the gilt cream. Apply solid copper on the flat circular sections of the turned design.

3 When the gilding has been completed, leave the candlestick for 15 minutes, then rub the surface very firmly all over with the clean cloth until it shines.

VELVET CUSHION

VELVET HAS A WARM, opulent look that is particularly appealing during the winter months. Making a few cushions is a quick way of transforming your room to reflect the changing of the seasons. Look for cheap velvet scraps and remnants at the local market for a real bargain, then combine the fabric with taffeta damask ribbon or edge a cushion with tasseled braid for a sensational effect. Adding special details such as buttonhole backs and velvet-covered buttons is well worth a little extra time. Alternatively, cover the buttons with contrasting taffeta or brocade and sew the ribbon border on the same side as the button band so that they become a feature and aren't hidden from view. The finished cushion measures 20 in (51 cm) square (including borders) and will fit a 16 in (40 cm) square cushion pad.

YOU WILL NEED
⅔ yd (60 cm) velvet, 56 in (140 cm) wide
Tape measure
Pins
Sewing thread
2 yds (1.9 m) ribbon, 1¼ in (3 cm) wide
Three 1 in (2.5 cm) easy-cover buttons
Scissors

1 Cut out a rectangle of velvet 47¼ × 21¼ in (120 × 54 cm). Turn under and pin a hem along both short ends of the rectangle, turning ⅔ in (1.5 cm), then 2 in (5 cm) to the wrong side. Stitch both hems in place.

2 Make three buttonholes placed centrally along one of the hemmed edges, the first buttonhole in the middle of the hem and a buttonhole 4 in (10 cm) either side of the central one.

5 Cut out circles of velvet using scraps and cover three buttons following the manufacturer's instructions. Stitch the buttons in place to correspond with the buttonholes to complete.

3 Mark the front of the cushion using pairs of pins along both long edges to indicate the fold lines, placing pins 9 in (23 cm) from the buttonhole hem edge and 13 in (33 cm) from the other hemmed edge. Cut the ribbon to make a square frame with inside edges of 15 in (38 cm), mitering the corners. Pin the ribbon onto the cushion front so the side edges are 1⅓ in (3.5 cm) from the fold lines and 2 in (5 cm) from the raw side edges. Stitch in place close to both sides of the ribbon.

4 With right sides facing, fold the cushion along the fold lines, folding the button band section first then the smaller buttonhole band section so that the hemmed edges overlap by 2 in (5 cm). Pin the sides and stitch. Trim the seams and corners then turn to the right side. Top-stitch a square within the ribbon frame to make the border.

Gifts

Devising different ways of wrapping gifts can be almost as exciting as unwrapping them on Christmas morning. A little imagination is required, so try not to leave all your wrapping until the last minute and choose wrapping to appeal to the recipient. Gather together a collection of ribbons, raffia, colored string, pinking shears, transparent tape and a selection of papers, from vibrantly colored tissue to metallic foils and iridescent cellophane. Display the presents in a tantalizing jumble at the base of the tree to create a focal point for the Christmas home.

CHRISTMAS SWEETS

SWEETS AND TREATS are part of the celebrations at Christmas and always make welcome gifts. With gift-giving becoming sometimes overshadowed by commercial pressures, it is worth the extra effort involved to make homemade goodies to give as gifts. The time and thought involved is sure to be appreciated by the friends and family members who receive them.

ABOVE: *Dried apricots and crystallized citrus fruits are wonderful combined with rich plain chocolate. The tart fruit flavors are perfectly complemented by the chocolate. Ready-to-eat apricots are available at most supermarkets and it is just a matter of dipping them into melted chocolate and allowing them to set. Use good quality chocolate for the dipping and pack the fruits into bags to give as presents.*

To crystallize fruit, remove the peel from three large, thin-skinned oranges in quarters. Boil the peel for 15 minutes in enough water to cover. Drain, cover with fresh cold water and boil again. Repeat until the peel is tender. Drain the peel again and cut into thin pieces.

Place 10 oz (275 g) sugar in a heavy-based saucepan with 5 fl oz (150 ml) water and stir over low heat to dissolve the sugar. Add the peel and boil for 35 minutes, until the syrup is completely absorbed. Drain once more in a strainer and then on paper for 12 hours.

Melt 8 oz (225 g) plain chocolate in a bowl over boiling water. Spear the peel pieces with toothpicks and dip them in chocolate. Leave them to set on baking parchment, then remove the toothpicks.

LEFT: *Repackaging bought sweets can make them look expensive and special enough to give as gifts. Chunks of nougat bought unwrapped by weight can be individually wrapped in lustrous cellophane, tied like bonbons and presented in decorated boxes tied with ribbon.*

BELOW: *Chocolate truffles are the ultimate decadent treat and make marvelous gifts when packaged into small boxes lined with waxed paper and colorful foil. Use plain chocolate with a high cocoa butter content (over 60 percent tastes best) and good quality cocoa powder for delicious results.*

10 oz (275 g) plain dark chocolate
2 oz (50 g) unsalted butter, cubed
½ pint (300 ml) heavy cream
   or crème fraîche
3 tbsp (45 ml) orange liqueur, dark rum
   or brandy
Plain dark chocolate and cocoa, for coating

Melt the chocolate, butter and cream together over low heat. The mixture should only be tepid. Stir in the liqueur but do not overmix. Pour into a shallow tray and refrigerate until firm.

Pull off teaspoon-sized lumps of the mixture and form into individual truffles without overworking the mixture to keep rough, uneven shapes. Melt the remaining chocolate and dip each truffle in the chocolate using two forks, then roll them immediately in the cocoa. Chill until set.

Store in an airtight container in the fridge for up to 2 weeks. This recipe makes about 30 truffles.

ABOVE: *Almond crescent cookies melt in the mouth and can be served when friends stop by during the festivities or given as presents packed into boxes tied with ribbon. Handle them with care as they are crumbly and break easily — you may be tempted to eat all the broken pieces!*

6 oz (175 g) unblanched almonds
¼ vanilla pod, roughly chopped
4 oz (100 g) superfine sugar
8 oz (225 g) unsalted butter
7 oz (200 g) all-purpose flour
½ tsp salt
Butter for greasing
Powdered sugar

Finely grind the almonds in a food processor and set to one side. Pulverize the vanilla pod with the sugar in a food processor. Cream the butter and vanilla sugar until light and fluffy. Mix the flour and salt and add it bit by bit to the butter mixture. Add the ground almonds and stir until the mixture forms a dough. Wrap the dough in cling film and refrigerate for at least an hour.

Preheat the oven to 350°F (180°C). Lightly butter two baking sheets. Pinch off walnut-sized pieces of dough and roll them on a floured surface into 2½ in (6 cm) long sausage shapes. Curve into crescents and place on the baking trays. Bake for 15—20 minutes until lightly colored. Leave to cool for 5 minutes, then carefully transfer to cool on a wire rack. When cool, dredge with powdered sugar and store in airtight containers. This recipe makes approximately 50 crescents.

WRAPPING PAPER AND GIFT TAGS

THERE ARE SO MANY WAYS in which to decorate wrapping paper, making it quite unnecessary to ever buy any again. Here is one of the simplest and quickest methods. This resist pattern is created by drawing a pattern on the paper with a candle. When the paper is washed over with a strong color, the paint avoids areas where the wax has been applied, thus leaving a lighter area in the form of the pattern. The only difficulty is that it can be quite hard to see the marks that you make with the candle, but this simply means that surprising patterns can be revealed when the paint is washed over the paper.

Cut out simple shapes from the patterned paper and stick them onto pieces of contrasting colored cardboard to make coordinating tags. Here the card has been trimmed with pinking shears to make a decorative edge.

YOU WILL NEED

Sheets of pale colored paper

Scrap paper to protect the work surface

White candle

Purple, orange and pink acrylic paint

Jam jar

Wide brush

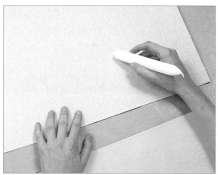

1 Lay the paper to be decorated on a smooth piece of scrap paper to protect the work surface. Draw your design on the paper by pressing really hard with the candle — this is easiest when the candle is cold.

2 Dilute the acrylic paint with water until it has the consistency of light cream. Brush the paint evenly across the surface of the paper to reveal the wax pattern. Lay the paper aside until the paint is dry.

Gift Wrapping Ideas

RIGHT: *Shiny gift bags with scalloped tops, made from thick paper and tied with ribbon, are ideal for awkward shaped gifts.*

BELOW: *Pannetone, the traditional Italian Christmas cake, is usually sold in an attractively printed box. Here it has been removed from its box, wrapped in a band of pink metallic crepe paper with gold ribbons and a generous piece of iridescent cellophane, making a simple but lovely gift.*

RIGHT: *This finely corrugated heavy paper lends itself to cutting, scoring and folding techniques and these small elliptically ended envelopes are an ideal project. The fold-over ends have been scored from behind to make the card bend easily. They make the perfect wrapping for silk scarves, ties or socks.*

RIGHT: *These brightly colored presents need no ribbons or bows. Leaves gathered from the garden in autumn and then pressed have been inserted between the colored paper wrapping and a matching cellophane top layer.*

BELOW: *This little paper cone has been made from two layers, the outer layer is patterned and the top made of glassine (a type of heavy colored wax paper). Simple to make and tied with an elegant ribbon, they make an ideal container for Christmas treats and delicacies.*

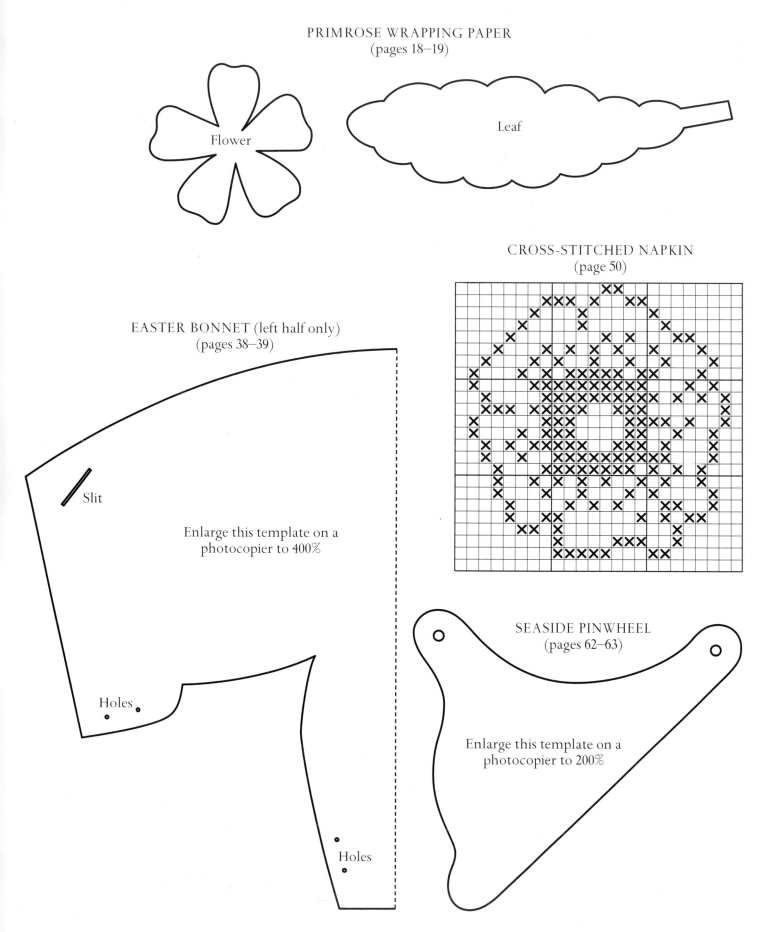

PRIMROSE WRAPPING PAPER
(pages 18–19)

Flower

Leaf

CROSS-STITCHED NAPKIN
(page 50)

EASTER BONNET (left half only)
(pages 38–39)

Slit

Enlarge this template on a
photocopier to 400%

Holes

Holes

SEASIDE PINWHEEL
(pages 62–63)

Enlarge this template on a
photocopier to 200%

PAPER CUTOUT TRAY (pages 22–25)

Tree

Place on fold

Bird

Enlarge this template on
a photocopier to 200%

PAPER CUTOUT CATS
(pages 106–107)

Enlarge this template on a
photocopier to 200%

Place on fold

Place on fold

CUT PAPER SHADE
(pages 170–171)

Butterfly

Flower

ORGANDY TABLECLOTH
(pages 72–73)

Enlarge this template on a
photocopier to 400%

STENCILED TABLECLOTH
(pages 40–41)

Enlarge this template on a
photocopier to 200%

MOTH-CUTOUT LANTERNS
(page 80)

Enlarge this template on a
photocopier to 200%

End

Repeat end border

Side

Repeat end border

CANVAS BEACH BAG
(pages 64–65)

Enlarge these templates on a photocopier to 400%

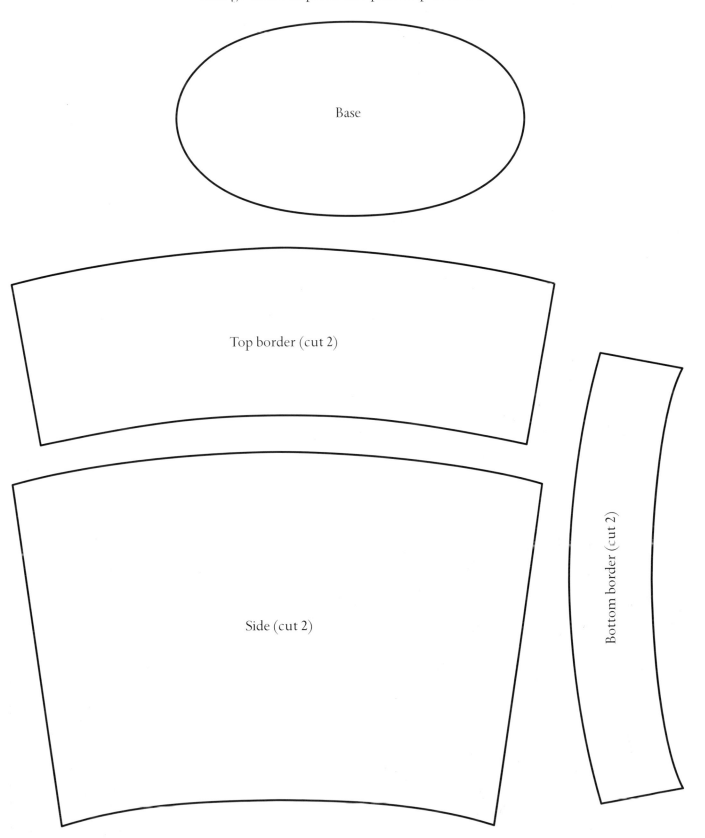

Base

Top border (cut 2)

Bottom border (cut 2)

Side (cut 2)

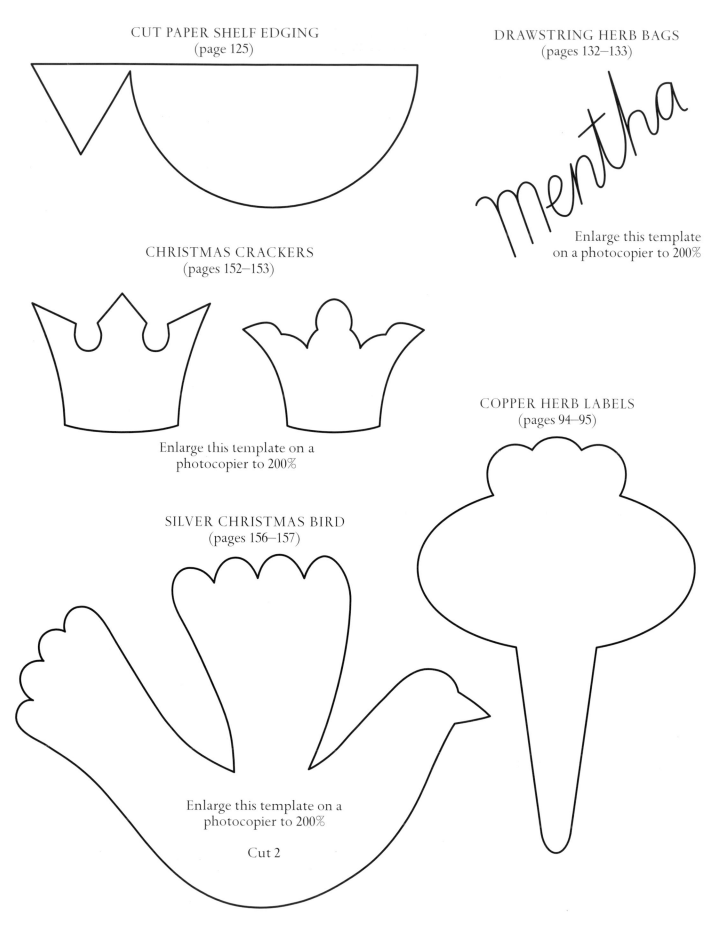

CUT PAPER SHELF EDGING
(page 125)

DRAWSTRING HERB BAGS
(pages 132–133)

Enlarge this template
on a photocopier to 200%

CHRISTMAS CRACKERS
(pages 152–153)

Enlarge this template on a
photocopier to 200%

COPPER HERB LABELS
(pages 94–95)

SILVER CHRISTMAS BIRD
(pages 156–157)

Enlarge this template on a
photocopier to 200%

Cut 2

PAINTED BIRD HOUSE
(pages 90–91)

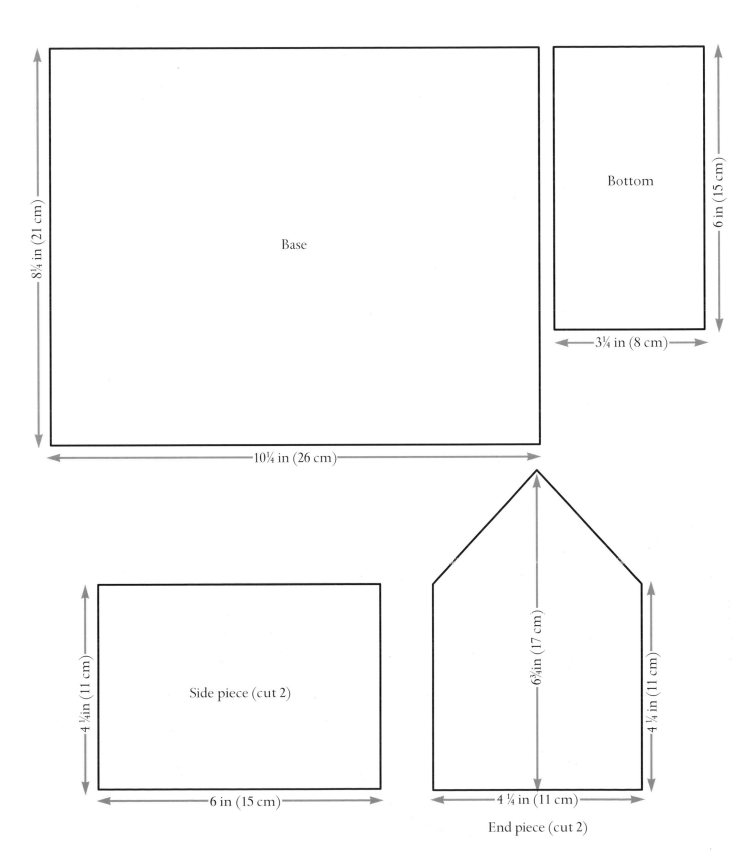

Base

8¼ in (21 cm)

10¼ in (26 cm)

Bottom

6 in (15 cm)

3¼ in (8 cm)

Side piece (cut 2)

4 ¼in (11 cm)

6 in (15 cm)

6¾in (17 cm)

4 ¼ in (11 cm)

4 ¼ in (11 cm)

End piece (cut 2)

SEED PACKETS
(pages 116–117)

EMBROIDERED TABLE MATS
(pages 150–151)

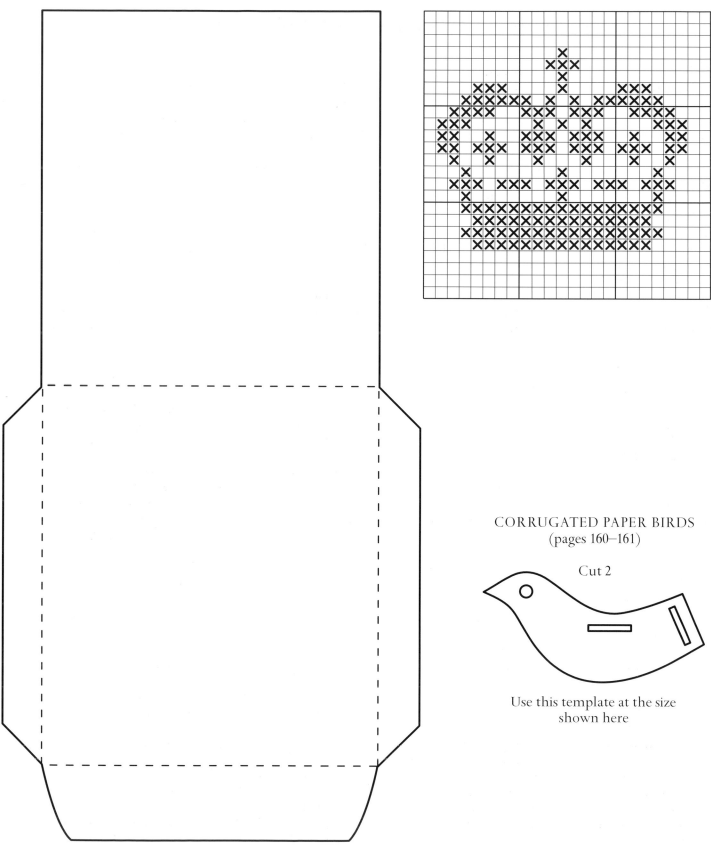

CORRUGATED PAPER BIRDS
(pages 160–161)

Cut 2

Use this template at the size
shown here

INDEX

Numbers in *italics* refer to photographs. Numbers in **boldface** refer to projects.